WITHDRAWN

HARVARD LIBRARY

WITHDRAWN

THE CULTURAL POLITICS OF RELIGIOUS CHANGE
A Study of the Sanoyea Kpelle in Liberia

Randolph Stakeman

African Studies
Volume 3

The Edwin Mellen Press
Lewiston Queenston

Library of Congress Cataloging-in-Publication Data

Stakeman, Randolph.
   The cultural politics of religious change.

   (African studies ; v. 3)
   Bibliography: p.
   Includes index.
   1. Kpelle (African people)--Religion.
2. Missions to Kpelle (African people) 3. Liberia--
Religion. I. Title. II Series: African studies
(Lewiston, N.Y.) ; v. 3.
BL2480.K72S72 1986   299'.683   86-23492
ISBN 0-88946-177-5

This is volume 3 in the continuing series
African Studies
Volume 3 ISBN 0-88946-177-5
AS Series ISBN 0-88946-175-9

Copyright © 1986, Randolph Stakeman.

All rights reserved. For information contact:

The Edwin Mellen Press   The Edwin Mellen Press
Box 450   Box 67
Lewiston, New York   Queenston, Ontario
USA 14092   LOS 1LO CANADA

Printed in the United States of America

TABLE OF CONTENTS

ACKNOWLEDGEMENTS iv

MAPS vi

INTRODUCTION 1

CHAPTER ONE
Kpelle Religion and Society 15

CHAPTER TWO
Sanoyea and the "Kwi" World 67

CHAPTER THREE
Religion and Politics 111

CHAPTER FOUR
The Sanoyea Mission 135

CHAPTER FIVE
Religious Change in Sanoyea 197

APPENDIX ONE
List of Informants 235

APPENDIX TWO
Evangelistic Report, Gbolomu 237

APPENDIX THREE
Twenty-six Lessons for Evangelists 241

SELECTED BIBLIOGRAPHY 243

INDEX 253

ACKNOWLEDGEMENTS

Academic research only exists because people have helped itinerant researchers along their way. I wish to thank those people who have helped me with friendship, assistance, financial support or simply a kind word. My research in Liberia was sponsored by an International Fellowships Fund Middle East and Africa grant. The Mabelle McLeod Lewis Foundation assisted with funds to support the writing of the dissertation on which this book is based. Various people have helped shelter two wanderers along the way: Nan Sedergren and Walter Greenough, Evelyn Stakeman, and especially Doretha Cooper and Pastor James and Anna Vankpana who took two fledglings under their wings in Liberia.

I have received aid in locating materials from Dr. Joel Lundeen, Rolf Charleston and the staff at the United Lutheran Church archive in Chicago; Augustine Jallah and his staff at the Republic of Liberia archive; Bishop Roland Payne, who allowed me to examine the Lutheran Church in Liberia archive, Dr. C. Rodney Armstrong and his staff at the University of Liberia library and Karen Fong of the Hoover Institute at Stanford.

I also wish to thank Mary Sherman, Vice President for Academic Affairs at the University of Liberia for all of her assistance. Fellow researchers Dr. James Gibbs, Dr. Svend Holsoe, Dr. Tom Shick, Dr. Ruth Stone and Dr. Verlon Stone all gave vital information to a "rookie" researcher. Paul Irwin and Richard Roberts provided invaluable criticism of this study when it was at the dissertation stage.

Most of all I want to thank the people of Sanoyea who gave of their time to be interviewed. I want to especially thank Peter Giddings, Amanda Gardiner and Alexander Mulbah for guiding me through the maze of Kpelle culture. Finally I want to thank my wife Catherine whose endurance and love made this work possible.

ETHNIC MAP OF LIBERIA

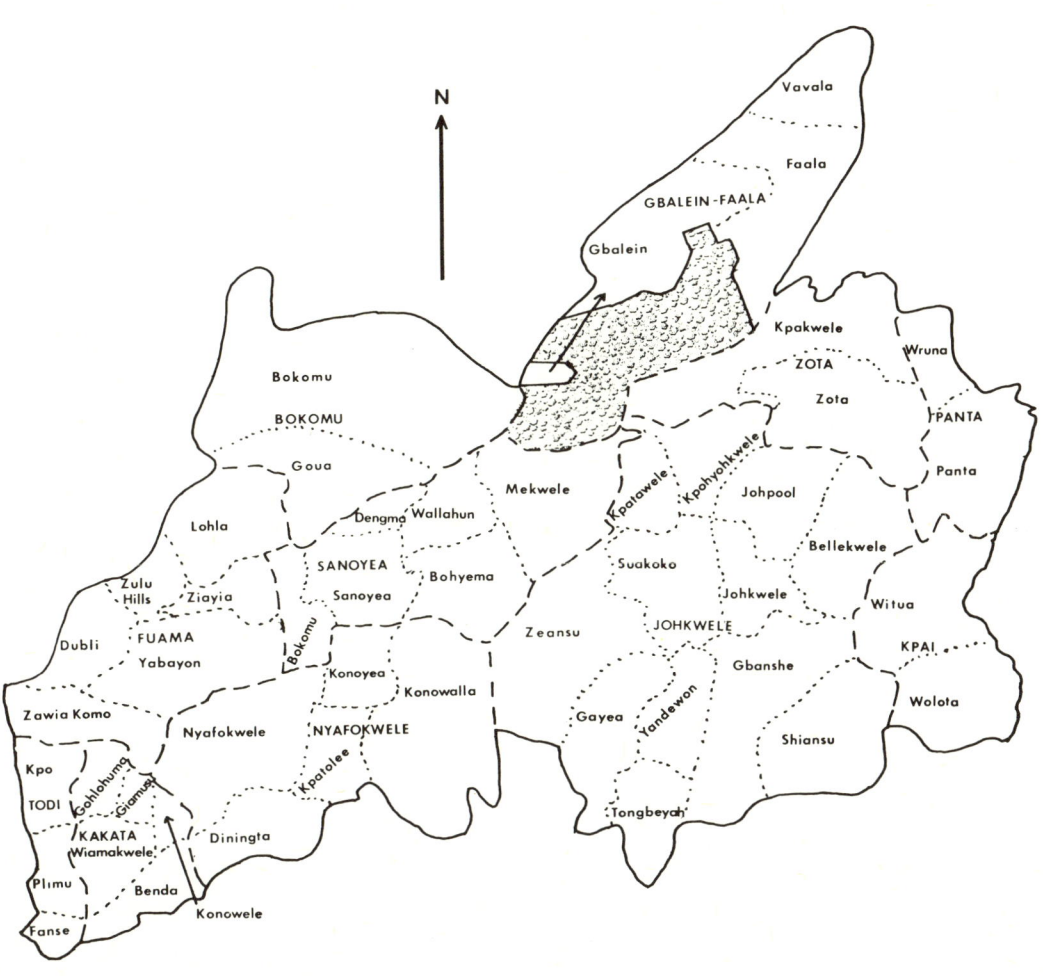

KPELLE CHIEFDOMS

Holsoe 1979 (after Siegmann 1978)

INTRODUCTION

African religion has seen a great deal of change in the 20th century. Centuries of contact with non African cultures and decades of colonialism have made religious syncretism and conversion to other religions vital areas of study. Millenarian movements and separatist churches arose in response to changing social and political circumstances. Islam and Christianity have spread to new areas of the continent and offered new alternatives to many people. The most dramatic occurrences of change, for example millenarianism, have received most of the scholarly attention until recently. Religious change, however, was not brought about only by ascetics, mystics and millenarians. More commonly the people who form the leading edge of religious change are those who quietly, almost imperceptibly, juggled and recombined various, often contradictory, religious ideas into new syntheses.

Conversion is only one possible result of the contact between African religions and Christianity or Islam. The same phenomena that lead some people to convert also subtly change the religious practices of those who do not convert. In this study I will look at the effects of Christianity on religious behavior, ritual performance and ideas about the supernatural among the Sanoyea Kpelle people of Liberia. I will use this case study to examine the relationship between religion and society and to investigate how religion changes in response to social change. I will focus on the period 1920-1958 when the Sanoyea chiefdom was simultaneously drawn into the Liberian state by political events and introduced to Christianity by Lutheran missionaries.

Religious change has more often been the subject of anthropological investigation than of historical research. The approach taken in this book builds upon, yet differs from current anthropological theory. I used the work of Robin Horton, J.D.Y. Peel and Monica Wilson on conversion as a starting point when looking at historical situations. These three works[1] only give one a starting point when looking at a specific historical situation.

I am especially indebted to the work of Victor Turner and Clifford Geertz for insights into the application of anthropological theory in historical situations. Turner views social action as a series of small social "dramas" in which people behave according to paradigms of social relations. At any given time several paradigms from past and present ideological systems are present in any culture. Individuals within a society can hold concurring or conflicting paradigms so that the the order which prevails at a given time results from the conflict of wills and intelligences.[2]

----

1. Robin Horton, "African Conversion," Africa 41 (1971): 87-108; and "On the Rationality of Conversion," Africa 45 (1975): 219-235, 373-399; J.D.Y. Peel, Aladura: A Religious Movement among the Yoruba, (London: Oxford University Press, 1969); Monica Wilson, Religion and the Transformation of Society, (London: Cambridge University Press, 1971.)

2. Victor Turner, Dramas, Fields and Metaphors, (Ithaca, N.Y.: Cornell University Press, 1974) pp.

This view of social behavior brings religious change into the historian's baliwick. The prevailing religious paradigms at a given point in time depend on the power relationships within a society and are subject to change. This is not to say that religion is simply a reflection of politics and power nor to apply some reductionsist, simplistic pseudo Marxist analysis to religion. Religious doctrine and religious explanatory systems have their own internal logics and integreties and are embedded in a whole series of social, family, and community relations. Religious change is the fascinating process by which a specifc historical situation affects all of these aspects of religion.

Religion is historical in another sense. As anthropologist Clifford Geertz has written, religion is a set of historically transmitted symbols, that is, a cultural system which affects behavior.[3] This cultural aspect of religion, religion's embodiment of a people's history and ideas of self, influenced how American missionaries and African villagers alike perceived and responded to different religions. Kpelle

----

14-15. For an interesting article on the implications of Turner's work for historians see Aylward Shorter, "Symbolism, Ritual and History: An examination of the work of Victor Turner," in Terence Ranger and Isariah Kimambo, The Historical Study of African Religion, (Berkeley: University of California Press, 1972) pp. 139-49.

3. Clifford Geertz, "Religion as a Cultural System, " in Michael Banton, Anthropological Approaches to the Study of Religion, (London: Tavistock Publications, 1966.)

religion, in other words, embodies "Kpelleness," the essentials of being a Kpelle, while Christianity embodied "western civilization" for the missionaries. Christianity was not just another religion during colonialism; it was the religion of the dominant minority. To participate in Christian rituals was to practice a foreign culture and often to forswear one's own culture. Such decisions were not made lightly. In order to understand these decisions one must look at how the goals and methods of Christian missionaries, the social and political ramifications of colonialism, and the actions of the local elites who mediated change, all shaped the nature and extent of religions change. An examination of these phenomena helps explain not only how religion changes, but also which parts of a religion change first, which members of a society change their religious behavior, and what hinders or promotes religious change.

The Kpelle and Liberia offer unique conditions for historical research on religious change. The Kpelle were chosen because of their importance in Liberia and their exposure to both Christianity and Islam during the twentieth century. The Kpelle are the largest ethnic group in Liberia, numbering over 200,000 or about twenty percent of the population.[4] Despite their importance in Liberia, little is known about the history of the Kpelle. What scholars do know comes from linguistic information and oral tradition. Liberia was settled by migrants from the Western

----

4. Willi Schulz, A New Geograhy of Liberia, (London: Longman Group Ltd., 1973,) p. 52.

Sudanic savannah, but the sequence, chronology and reasons for the migrations are points of debate.

Most historians agree that the first migrants into what is now Liberia belonged to the Kwa and Western Atlantic language groups and arrived sometime between 1000 and 1450.[5] The Kpelle entered Liberia through Guinea as part of the great fourteenth through sixteenth century movement of Mande speakers throughout West Africa as the empires of first Mali and then Songhai declined. The Kpelle probably reached their present location in Bong County, Liberia shortly before 1600.[6] Their oral traditions tell of a huge town called Wyeta in the modern Zota or Jokwelle Chiefdoms.[7] From Wyeta the Kpelle dispersed westward to the St. Paul River and by the nineteenth century the continued Kpelle expansion westward across the river and southwestward along the river was the most important population movement in central Liberia. These migrations continued into the twentieth century as the Kpelle form autonomous chiefdoms throughout the area.[8]

Liberia's unique history makes it an excellent

----

5. See Yves Person, "Les Kissi et leurs statuettes de pierre dans la cadre de l'historie ouest-africaine," Bulletin I.F.A.N. 23 (1961).

6. Willi Schulz, A New Geography of Liberia, p. 47.

7. Bai T. Moore, Tribes of the Western Province and Denwoin People, (Monrovia: Department of the Interior, Republic of Liberia, 1955) p. 34.

8. Willi Schulz, A New Geography of Liberia, p. 47.

place to study the effects of missions on African religious behavior. The modern Liberian state was founded by a group of free black emigrants from the United States sponsored by the American Colonization Society. The Society received funding and assistance from the United States government, a group of white philanthropists and some slaveowners who feared the growth of a free black population especially in the south. Although the major objective of colonization was to solve America's racial problems, the spread of Christianity was also an important goal. Many of the leaders of the movement defended the program and tried to solicit funds by emphasizing the evangelistic elements of colonization,

> Every company of emigrants sent out by this colonization society may be regarded as a band of missionaries. They go to that country with some knowledge of the Gospel; they are accompanied by intelligent ministers of Christ; they form there a Christian society where all the advantages of civilized and Christianized institutions are exemplified, and which become a bright and powerful center of civilization and religion. How mighty must be the influence of such a minister and such congregations upon the surrounding nations and tribes of heathens! how rapid will be the triumphs of the gospel in such circumstances.[9]

----

9. [Henry Clay], Address to the Clergy of All Denominations, (Albany: Packard and van Benthuysen,

Colonization proponents argued that the colonists' race would make them the ideal missionaries for Africa. Not only would they be more resistant to the diseases which made West Africa "the white man's grave," the colonists were also believed to share a common heritage with the indigenous people:

> Africans themselves or at least [with] African blood, will not all their feelings, all their best affections, induce them to seek the good of their countrymen?[10]

The opponents of colonization answered this question with a resounding "No!" They argued that race had little to do with what they saw as the general failure of colonization to spread Christianity anywhere in the world. They noted that,

> Christian colonization has either uniformly wrought the extermination of the aborigines, or that it tends to do so, except where the Colonists themselves lapse into barbarism.[11]

These authors, Cornish and Wright, predicted that the

1824).

10. Henry Clay, "Speech at the 31st anniversary of the American Colonization Society, Washington, January 18, 1848," in Remarks on the Colonization of the Western Coast of Africa, (N.Y.: W.L. Burroughs Steam Power Press, 1850), p. 21.

11. Samuel Cornish and Theodore Wright, The Colonization Scheme Considered in its rejection by the colored People, (Newark: Aaron Quest, 1840).

colonists would assume a superiority to the indigenes and that -intent upon their own concerns- they would interact with the local people only as it served their own interests and convenience.[12] Unfortunately the anti-colonization arguments would prove closer to the truth.

The evangelical roots of the colonization scheme did, however, have long term effects. From its inception the colony remained open to missions and missionaries who wanted to go there. A connection developed between church membership and the most important political positions within the colony. Political factions organized around religious sectarian groups and several Liberian presidents were ministers or held important church offices. Most important for this study, the missionary aspects of the colony's founding reinforced the colonists feeling of cultural superioirty toward the indigenous people. The colonists saw themselves as the bringers of "civilization and culture" to Africa and used evangelization to validate their own self interests.[13]

Throughout the 19th century the Americo Libereian settlers eked out a living in agricultural communities.[14] Dependent upon European imports and

----

12. Cornish and Wright, The Colonization Scheme.

13. Tom W. Shick, Behold the Promised Land, (Baltimore: Johns Hopkins University Press, 1977, 1980) p. 64.

14. See Tom W. Shick, Behold the Promised Land, for a detailed study of the nineteenth century Americo

with only a small exportable surplus, the small state continually found itself in financial difficulty. The young republic, beset with economic woes and preoccupied with internal political strife, remained confined to the coast until the late 19th century.[15]

Although the settlers developed ties with the African peoples near the coast, contacts with the hinterland peoples like the Kpelle remained sporadic. Interaction between the Kpelle and the Liberian settlements was at first limited to Liberian explorers and adventurous traders. Liberia did not solidify ties with the hinterland until faced with French and British challenges to its territorial claims. In the first decades of the 20th century Liberia moved to establish control over the hinterland people and this movement brought them into contact with the Kpelle. One by one the Kpelle chiefdoms were made part of the Liberian state either through treaty or through warfare.

Incorporation into the Liberian state brought the Kpelle into contact not only with different political and economic systems, but also with Christian missionaries. Historians are only beginning to understand the complexities of the encounters between Christian missionary and African villager. In these encounters people from different cultures, for whom religion formed a major part of daily life, met under

----
Liberian community.

15. The most detailed study of Liberia's financial woes is George W. Brown, The Economic History of Liberia, (Washington, D.C.: The Associated Publishers Inc., 1941).

the unique conditions of colonialism. Historians are now examining this encounter as an interaction between different theologies, rituals, myths and symbols, in short, between different religious systems. Historians have been challenged to apply social and anthropological techniques to a reexamination of the misssionaries themselves.[16] What did the missionaries actually preach and teach in Africa? How were they organized? Were there differences in the evangelistic methods and theologies of the different sects? What theories and strategies of conversion lay behind the mission's efforts? What was the role of education in the evangelistic process and what kinds of education did the mission attempt? What were the relationships between the colonial government and the mission? How did mission policies adapt to village life and African culture?

Sanoyea chiefdom in Liberia offers an excellent place to try to answer such questions. The Lutheran mission arrived in Sanoyea in 1917 only five years after the Liberian government had "pacified" the area. The mission remained active until 1965 making Sanoyea the oldest continually staffed mission station among the Kpelle. Sanoyea's political leaders "collaborated" with the Liberian government so that the chiefdom became open to "outside" influences.

Although the focus will be on one chiefdom, the research for this study comes from several sources.

----

16. Thomas O. Beidelman, "Social Theory and the Study of Christian Missions," <u>Africa</u> 44,3 (1974): 237-249.

Policy decisions made by Lutheran church officials in New York City, on the spot decisions by African evangelists in small hamlets, and countless daily choices made by Kpelle men and women have all contributed to Kpelle religious history. The major source for this volume has been the Kpelle people themselves. Field work was conducted in Sanoyea and Monrovia in 1976 and 1977. Interviews with evangelists, a Koranic teacher, Poro secret society officials, elders and other lay people form the core of this study. The interviews elicited information about the informant's life and background, how and why his family immigrated into the area, local history, religious practices before and after the mission came, the activities and attitudes of the missionaries and other subjects depending upon the informant's special expertise. About half of the interviews were conducted in English and the rest in Kpelle through an interpreter. Follow up interviews were conducted when points needed further clarification, when information contradicted or disagreed with other sources and when an informant proved especially knowledgable.

The first accounts of the missions were written by the missionaries themselves. These books had exotic titles and were generally aimed at soliciting funds from people back home. Books like <u>Ethiopia: Her Gloom and her Glory</u>, <u>Day Dawn in Africa</u>, <u>A Lone Woman on the African Coast</u>, and <u>Liberian Oddessey: By Hammock and Surfboat</u>, all contained accounts of mission life in

Liberia.[17] These books told of the missionaries' hardships, the difficulties ahead, their small successes, and what one might call the "white Christian's burden," that is, their duty to convert the "heathen." Despite the prejudices in these works they do contain some useful information. These missionaries provide eyewitness accounts of African religious practices even though the missionaries often misunderstood what they saw and only saw part of what was happening around them.

I have used missionary accounts in published articles and unpublished documents from both Liberia and the United States. The Lutheran mission published periodicals to inform the people in the United States about their work and to solicit funds. The most important periodical, The Foreign Missionary, contains regular progress reports from all of the Lutheran church foreign missions. The Liberian articles provide accounts of Kpelle ritual as well as stories of missionaries' tribulations and successes. The United Lutheran Church archive in Chicago, the Lutheran Church in Liberia archive and the records kept at the Sanoyea Mission Station provided insight into the internal working of the mission. The articles written by the missionaries and the archival material provide evidence

----

17. David Christy, Ethiopia, Her Gloom and Glory, (Cinncinati: Rickey, Mallory, Webb, 1857), Anna M. Scott, Day Dawn in Africa, (N.Y.: Protestant Episcopal Society for the Promotion of Evangelical Knowledge, 1858), Agnes McCallister, A Lone Woman on the African Coast, (N.Y.: Hunt and Easton, 1896), Frederick Price, Liberian Oddessey: By Hammock and Surfboat, (N.Y.: Pageant Press, 1954).

of the missionary attitudes toward the Kpelle and their culture.

This study has also used ethnologies as historical documents. Ethnologists worked in this area of Liberia at a relatively early date as a result of mission sponsored attempts to study the Kpelle language. Diedrich Westermann's 1913 study and William Welmers's late 1940's study were especially important as a basis for historical comparisons of Kpelle social and religious practices.[18] The ethnologies served as evidence that certain practices were indeed present at certain times and helped provide a chronology for the oral data. Whenever possible written records and oral information were checked against each other in order to verify events. The Liberian National Archive and published travelers' accounts provided additional information.

I begin this study with an examination of the relationship between Kpelle religion and society to see how each reflects and influences the other. The second and third chapters look at the history of the town of Sanoyea to see how the political and social context affects religious change. The fourth chapter focuses on the mission and its attempts to alter Kpelle religion. The fifth chapter will examine the impact of the mission on Kpelle religion and society.

----

18. Diedrich Westermann, Die Kpelle, (Gottingen, 1921) and William Welmers, Spoken Kpelle, (N.Y.: Lutheran Church, 1950).

CHAPTER ONE

Kpelle Religion and Society c.1900-1958

Social change and religious change are intimately related among the Kpelle and neither kind of change can be truly understood without examining the other. This study will focus on Sanoyea chiefdom, a medium sized Kpelle chiefdom where the Lutherans concentrated much of their missionary work. I will examine Kpelle religion from the emergence of the Sanoyea chiefdom at the turn of the century to 1958, when the founding family declined in importance. This is a period when the Kpelle were drawn more closely into the Liberian state and Christianity became an important religious option for the Kpelle.

Although the chiefdom of Sanoyea underwent important changes during this period, changes that are reflected and influenced by Kpelle religion, several things remained the same. The agricultural mode of production remained dominant and the landowning elite managed to retain control of production, although new crops and markets allowed new people to enter the ruling elite. The conflict between the society's emphasis on social group allegiance and individual achievement continued throughout the period. As we shall see the Kpelle world view and religious behavior mirror and influence this conflict. The Kpelle also continued to view the supernatural as something one can and must manipulate for protection and individual advantage. The options available to people, the way people use them, and the social costs of these options do change and as we shall see these religious changes result from social changes and the presence of Christianity.

This chapter offers an introduction to the grammar and vocabulary of Kpelle religion, that is, its principles of operation and the various entities and beings it contains. I will begin by briefly considering some of the theoretical problems in this kind of study. I will then examine the relationship between Kpelle religion and Kpelle social organization to see how religion was used to support the social stratification system and to integrate social groups. I will discuss how Kpelle religion reflected and embodied Kpelle social tensions. Finally, I will examine the options available to the Kpelle within Kpelle "traditional" religion. In this chapter I will explain what the options were during the period under discussion. In later chapters I will look at how and why the options have changed as a result of social changes.

For the purposes of this study I take religion to be a belief in a transcendent reality containing supernatural beings, powers and agencies which affect human beings and natural processes in the common sense world.[1] The subjective and introspective nature of

----

1. Any definition of religion creates controversy. For example, not all scholars agree that a belief in supernatural beings is a necessary condition for a religious belief. I have chosen this one because it seems to fit the Kpelle case. For other definitions and a discussion of the problems in defining religion see Clifford Geertz, "Religion as a Cultural System," and Melford Spiro, "Religion: Problems of Definition

religious belief makes it a difficult subject for historical research. Much of the writing on African conversion to Islam and Christianity has concentrated on whether people "truly believe" in Islam or Christianity. For the historian this raises unverifiable questions and as Robin Horton has pointed out it has resulted in much unproductive scholarship.[2] This study will therefore focus on religious behavior not religious belief. Religious behavior is the participation in the rituals and practices associated with religious belief regardless of whether the participants actually accept those beliefs. In this study I consider a person a Christian if he participates in the Christian rituals, a Muslim if he participates in the Muslim rituals, and so on. The question whether an individual actually believes in the religion he practices is of secondary importance for me as long as that person behaves as if he believes.

In order to find meaning individuals postulate a plan of how the world operates that goes beyond surface appearances. Religion attributes events to causes ranging from broken taboos, to the actions of ghosts and gods, to predestination. This is what Clifford Geertz has called a model "of" reality.[3] Religion not

----

and Explanation," both in Anthropological Approaches to the Study of Religion, ed. Michael Banton (London: Tavistock Publications Limited, 1968).

2. See Robin Horton, "On the Rationality of Conversion," Africa 45 (1975): 219-235.

3. Geertz, "Religion as a Cultural System," p. 3.

only offers a model of reality, it also offers a model "for" reality, that is, a plan for living in the world and coping with daily life.[4] Anthropologists from Edward Tylor to Robin Horton have compared religion's role in non-Western societies to science's role in our own.[5] Religion provides the technical mastery over the environment which science provides for us. If breaking taboos causes crops to fail, then one can assure success by avoiding the breaking of taboos. If offerings to a spirit can cure infertility, then one knows how to become fertile.

Tylor and Horton are to some extent correct, but religion does more than provide some sense of mastery over one's environment. People also use religion to achieve larger goals like salvation or acceptance into a social group which go beyond the role science plays. Religion can use methods like prayer and meditation which go past the manipulation of earthly materials. Religion, while providing an explanatory system much as science does in our society, also does much more.

To understand what religion does in a society one has first to look at the question of the relationship between religion and society. Various people have tried to explain the relationship between religion and the social system of which it is a part. For Emile Durkheim religion is "a system of ideas with which

----

4. Geertz, "Religion as a Cultural System," p. 7

5. See Edward Tylor, Primitive Culture and Robin Horton, "African Traditional Thought and Western Science," Africa 37 (1967): 50-71,155-187.

individuals represent to themselves the society of which they are members, and the obscure but intimate relations which they have with it."[6] Once a religion has developed, it loses its character as a human creation to become an objective reality confronting succeeding generations, so that, "the productions of the human brain appear as independent beings endowed with life and entering into relation both with one another and the human race.[7] Religion can thus act upon society to shape human action as Weber has pointed out.[8] Religion and society are therefore neither independent nor simply reflective of each other. They rather form a dialectic with each acting upon the other.[9] As Geertz explains,

> In religious belief and practice a group's ethos [the tone, character, and quality of their life, its moral and aesthetic style and mood] is rendered intellectually reasonable by being shown to represent a way of life ideally adapted to the actual state of affairs the world view [the model of reality]

----

6. Emile Durkheim, <u>The Elementary Forms of the Religious Life</u>, (New York: The Free Press, 1965), p. 257.

7. Karl Marx, <u>Capital</u> vol. 1, (N.Y.: Random House, Modern Library edition, 1906), p. 83.

8. Max Weber, <u>The Protestant Ethic and the Spirit of Capitalism</u> (New York: Charles Scribner's Sons, 1958) pp. 155-183.

9. Peter L. Berger, <u>The Sacred Canopy</u> (Garden City, N.Y.: Doubleday and Company, Anchor Books edition, 1969), pp.40-41.

describes, while the world view is rendered emotionally convincing by being presented as an image of an actual state of affairs peculiarly well arranged to accomodate such a way of life.[10]

The relationship between a way of life and a world view does not remain constant. Although a society usually seeks to preserve an outward appearance of continuity, both society and religion change. Shifts in the relationship between the two occur when individual goals do not mesh with the methods and explanations a particular world view entails. At this point people will start to make their lives conform to their religion or their religion conform to their lives or both. The relationship between a religion and its social context therefore must form the background to any understanding of religious change.

The Kpelle really have two intertwined social systems: a kinship based system and a "big man" system based on patron/client relationships. I will first look at how each of these systems is related to the material base of Kpelle society. Although each system will be discussed separately, one must always bear in mind that they occur concurrently. Individuals may achieve high status in both at the same time or in one but not the other. I will then discuss how Kpelle religious beliefs reflect and affect these social and economic relations. In so doing I am not assuming that these systems represent an unchanging social

----

10. Geertz, "Religion as a Cultural System," p. 3.

structure. On the contrary, they represent the cumulative effects of the historical processes I will discuss in the next chapter.

Unfortunately few historians have worked among the Kpelle and there is not enough information to present a detailed historical overview of all the Kpelle chiefdoms which had developed by the 19th century. The Kpelle were located so far inland that few reports of their activities reached European traders along the coast. Until more Kpelle oral histories are collected on a systematic basis, almost nothing will be known about them during the 16th through 18th centuries.[11] More research has been done on the Kpelle during the 19th and 20th centuries.[12]

----

11. A collection of oral traditions in Western Liberia contains only a few Kpelle traditions. See Bai T. Moore, Tribes of the Western Tribes and Denwoin People, (Monrovia: Interior Department, Republic of Liberia, 1955.)

12. For the 19th century the best sources are Willi Schulz's work on iron smelting, "Early Iron Smelting among the Northern Kpelle," Liberian Studies Journal 3 (1970-71) and Richard Fulton's reconstruction of Kpelle state organization, "The Kpelle Traditional Political System, Liberian Studies Journal 1 (1968) and "The Political Structure and Function of the Poro in Kpelle Society," American Anthropologist 74 (1972). Two anthropological studies were especially helpful for the twentieth century social history. Parts of Diedrich Westermann's 1913 study of Fuama chiefdom (a chiefdom on Sanoyea's western border) have been translated from the German in James Sibley and Diedrich Westermann, LIBERIA OLD AND NEW, (Garden City, N.Y.: Doubleday and Company, 1928). William Welmers' ethnology based on Sanoyea, Spoken Kpelle, (N.Y.: Lutheran Church, 1950) was also helpful.

To understand Kpelle religion we must first start with a brief historical overview of the material bases of Kpelle society. The Kpelle had an ironworking technology when they arrived in Liberia in the 16th century. Several iron smelting sites have been found in the northern Kpelle chiefdoms. Although iron was traded to other Liberian groups for locally produced cloth and brass jewelry, its major economic importance was in the manufacture of tools and weapons.[13] Iron tools enabled the Kpelle to farm and migrate in the forests of Liberia. By the end of the 19th century the Kpelle had formed some 30 to 50 autonomous chiefdoms in central Liberia.[14] All sources indicate that most Kpelle, including the Sanoyea Kpelle, have been predominantly agriculturalists at least since the 19th century. Although new crops have been introduced from time to time, rice has been and remains the major food crop and staple of the Kpelle diet. The Kpelle also grow garden crops like green leafy vegetables, cassava, okra, plaintain, and sweet potatoes. The Kpelle cultivate the oil palm tree from which edible palm oil is obtained. During the 19th century they were also cash crop producers cultivating kola nuts for trade to the Muslims in nearby Guinea.[15]

The arrival of the Americo Liberians along the coast at first had little effect on the Kpelle, but by

----

13. Willi Schulz, <u>A New Geography of Liberia</u>, p 155.

14. Richard Fulton, "The Political Structure and Function of the Poro," p. 1220.

15. Interview with Bangali Donso, May 26, 1977.

the last quarter of the 19th century the southern Kpelle were supplying foodstuffs and labor to the Americo Liberians.[16] The Liberian government's 1910-20 conquest of the Kpelle brought them more fully into the Liberian economic sphere, but did not change the economic base. The Kpelle would occasionally work on Americo Liberian farms and plantation but they continued to be predominantly subsistence farmers. After World War II the Kpelle also sold cash crops like rubber and coffee to the Americo Liberians.[17]

The Kpelle engaged in other economic activites as well. They supplemented their rice diet by hunting and fishing. Game is now becoming scarce in the Sanoyea area, but earlier in the 20th century larger game- like elephant- was common. The Kpelle also had access to fresh water fishing grounds because of their proximity to the St. Paul River and its tributaries. The Sanoyea Kpelle rarely kept livestock other than chickens.

Despite these other activities, rice farming was the major productive activity and agriculture dominated Kpelle social relations. Access to land and the control of labor are the keys to the Kpelle mode of production. Not only did the Kpelle need the use of large areas for their extensive, slash and burn, shifting cultivation techniques, they also needed

----

16. See Chapter 2 below.

17. For the story of one such rubber grower see interview with D.B. Livingstone, June 14, 1977. For a short overview of rubber and coffee cultivation in Liberia see Willi Schulz, <u>A New Geography of Liberia</u>, pp 113-26.

access to fertile hunting and fishing grounds. The importance of land in social relations can best be seen by tracing a typical settlement pattern.[18] The first people to settle on unclaimed land became the "owners of the land." Subsequent settlers had to ask permission to work the land. Once permission was granted that family could usually continue to use that land even if they allowed it to lie fallow for several years. Thus, a settlement came to be made up of several landholding patrilineages.

Kpelle lineages in Sanoyea seldom acted as corporate units, nor did they contain a complex system of social differentiation. The elders of these lineages however did wield much power within Kpelle society because lineages controlled access to land. Each individual had a right to use some of the land his patrilineage controlled. In practice several non-kinspeople could be adopted into the lineage or become clients of lineage leaders. When an area was first settled, one lineage would own most of the land and make most of the decisions about its use. As population density increased the situation changed. Even though the one lineage remained the "owner of the land" such decisions concerned all the elders of the community. Nominally the decision was made by the local chief, but the land was something held in trust for the community and the oldest and most important

----

18. The following description is based upon Fulton's "The Traditional Kpelle Political System," and interviews with several informants including, Peter Giddings, James Cooper, Benjamin Barclay and Mulbah Dangolu.

members of the leading families participated in the decision. As early as 1913 Westermann had observed:

> the king [chief] is not more than the executor of the tribal will as expressed by the adult free men, led by the clan heads. Without their consent he cannot decide any important matter and the initiative in questions concerning public welfare lies no less with the elders than with the king himself.[19]

Usually the "owner of the land" lineage remained an important family and had an important say in the disposition of land. Indeed, one measure of the power of the founding lineage was its ability to maintain control over land decisions.

Labor is the second important means of production to consider and kinship relations define the labor force. The domestic household usually contains a man, his wives, their children and perhaps the man's brother or mother. All members of the household help in its labor requirements and additional labor can be drawn from the wider kinship group. A person has obligations to work for certain elder members of his lineage. These will include his father, mother, father's brother, mother's brother, grandparents, mother's mother's brother, father's mother's brother and father's father's brother. A man has reciprocal labor

----

19. Sibley and Westermann, Liberia Old and New, p. 150.

obligations with his siblings.[20] If a project calls for more labor than his kin can provide, a person will probably join a cooperative work group (kuu). These groups will go from one member's farm to another's generally performing heavy work.

Kpelle marriages are often based upon affection, but they are also symbiotic economic relationships between men and women. Men and women need each other's assistance to perform the tasks necessary for subsistence. In Kpelle rice cultivation men perform only the initial land clearing operations.[21] They cut down the large vegetation and burn the land both to clear it and to provide some fertilization. After this preparation the farm work is entirely in the hands of the women and children. Women plant, weed, tend to the rice and play a large role in the harvesting. Women not only perform most of the manual labor in rice production, they manage the domestic work force, maintain the household and usually control the use of the harvest.

Women are a source of labor in other ways as well. Through marriage and the family, women are essential in bringing new labor into a lineage.

----

20. Beryl Bellman, Village of Curers and Assassins, (The Hague: Mouton Press, 1975) pp. 181-185.

21. Conversations with Anna Vankpana and a women's kuu leader. Also see James Gibbs, "The Kpelle of Liberia," in Peoples of Africa, ed. James L. Gibbs (New York: Holt, Rinehart and Winston, 1965) and Caroline Bledsoe, Women and Marriage in Kpelle Society, (Stanford: Stanford University Press, 1980.

Marriage in Kpelle society calls for a payment of bridewealth to the bride's family. Among the Kpelle this often involved a transfer of labor. The groom would often agree to work for the bride's family in lieu of a payment in cash or goods.[22] After a few years, if the husband had proven himself a good worker, he and his wife could start their own household.[23] As the bearers of children women are central to the reproduction of the labor force. In Kpelle marriage a woman's first one or two children were often affiliated to the husband's parents' household rather than her own. Subsequent children became part of the woman's own household.[24]

Women clearly hold a subordinate position in Kpelle society. Men control all legal rights to women and exclude women from all formal political positions. It is extremely difficult for women to become wealthy in their own right because they can legally control the labor of others only through men. Women's crucial economic importance, however, allowed them to exercise informal power by withholding or bestowing their economic services. For example, a woman could refuse to cook for her husband if she felt he was abusing her. On the other hand she could give food to bachelors or other males to obtain favors from

----

22. Interview with Charles Wellington, April 21, 1977.
23. Interview with Amanda Gardiner, March 3, 1977.
24. Interview with Amanda Gardiner, March 3, 1977.

them.[25]

Before the Liberian government banned slavery in 1930, slaves were another potential source of labor. Kpelleland was the scene for numerous wars during the 19th and early 20th centuries. War captives were taken by the Kpelle for use as domestic slaves or for sale to European and African slavers. In addition, the Kpelle practiced a system of pawning. A person's labor- usually a child's- was used to settle a debt or as security for a loan. The pawn lived and worked for the household holding him. Many pawns were not redeemed until adulthood while others were never redeemed. Although this practice was banned along with slavery, the Kpelle continued to pawn.[26]

Within the kinship based social system the elders controlled the important economic resources- land and women. They exercised this control through religious secret societies- the male Poro Society and the female Sande Society.[27] The Poro (male) and Sande (female) secret societies embody Kpelle civil law, sacred

----

25. Caroline Bledsoe, Women and Marriage in Kpelle Society, (Stanford: Stanford University Press, 1980), p. 113.

26. Interview with Peter Giddings, January 19, 1977.

27. Similar secret societies are found in other parts of West Africa. Kenneth Little has done extensive work on these societies among the Mende in neighboring Sierra Leone. See especially, "The Role of the Secret Society in Cultural Specialization," American Anthropologist 51:199-212 and "The Political Function of the Poro" Africa 35 (1965) 349-65 and 36 (1966) 62-72.

communal ties, and codes of ethical behavior. Almost all Sanoyea Kpelle belonged to the secret societies because participation in community affairs depended on membership,

> The idea of initiation is that it is instructive, it's tuitional, and you must be educated to the knowledge of the affairs of the kingdom. Consequently you don't have to be told your duty, It's inherent in you. So at a certain age, the age of discretion, of maturity, you become a member... [a non-initiate] is irresponsible, very irresponsible in speech, in attitude, and in action. He is unreliable, there is nothing for you to bind him to, he's slippery.[28]

The Poro's sacred forest grove was a place to communicate with the community's ancestors.[29] The ancestors transmitted their store of knowledge to their descendants through the Poro, thus reaffirming the connection between the living and the dead. Masks of local heroes or caricatures of half human and half animal faces represented Poro offices. A spirit inhabited each mask and possessed the wearer. The

----

28. Interview with Dougba Carranda, December 29, 1976.

29. In his classic work on ancient Greece and Rome Fustel de Coulange similarly describes the ancient cities as both collections of families and associations of their ancestral shrines. See Numa Denis Fustel de Coulange, The Ancient City, (Garden City, N.Y.: Doubleday and Company, Anchor Books edition, n.d.), pp.126-155.

spirit, not the wearer, performed any Poro actions, thus giving supernatural sanction to the Poro's official acts. Poro officials spoke with the wisdom, authority and sanction of the community and the ancestors. Through its frightening masked figures, the Poro gave concrete form to the spirit world.[30] The social and religious systems reinforced each other through the supernatural sanctions of the Poro. All Poro members swore to uphold the decisions of the Poro elders. This made all members of the community, including chiefs, subject to the Poro leaders in Poro matters.[31] The definition of Poro matters could be stretched to include many things, and in practice they included community law transgressions like bloodletting, incest and arson. The Poro also acted as a court to hear cases in which Poro rules had been violated and to punish anyone who had revealed Poro secrets.[32]

The Poro was the major repository of Kpelle knowledge and the elders of the community- who are

----

30. George W. Harley, "Notes on the Poro in Liberia," Papers of the Peabody Museum of American Archaeology and Ethnography 19,2 (1941): 7, 13.

31. Sibley and Westermann, Liberia Old And New, p. 151.

32. William Welmers, "Secret Medicines, Magic and Rites of the Kpelle Tribe of Liberia" Southwestern Journal of Anthropology 5 (1949): 234-235 and Spoken Kpelle, (Liberia: Lutheran Church in Liberia,1948) Unit 20, pp. 2-4.

closest to the ancestors- controlled it.[33] The Poro operated an initiation school to instill Poro values in youngsters at an impressionable age. This control over the socialization process allowed the Poro to maintain cultural attitudes, affirm the authority of the community's elders, and to teach the Kpelle achievement ethic and model of reality. As Sanoyea's first full time missionary self-righteously wrote in 1919,

> the only near imitation of a school known in the life of the real native man...is a school of superstition and unbelief, of black arts, of witchcraft and spirit worship, of ancestor worship and aloofness from God...if the spirits and our dead ancestors help us to become rich and influential here -mighty to lord it over others and make them our slaves, we will be so much better off when we go back to God... All is what their old people learned to be good to help people on in this world, whether fetishes or charms to aid people in cheating, stealing and gambling, or

----

33. Claude Meillassoux contends that in West African agricultural societies, the elders maintain their control over the young by controlling access to women through the bridewealth system and technical knowledge. Although the Kpelle Poro might at first seem like a good example of this process, anthropologist Caroline Bledsoe found that the Poro and Sande societies actually taught little that was not common knowledge. More important than what was taught is the Kpelle belief that the Poro elders control some esoteric knowledge. See Meillassoux. "From Reproduction to Production," Economy and Society 1 (1972) 93-105 and Bledsoe, Women and Marriage in Kpelle Society, p. 69.

whatever way anyone has heard as having made men rich or respected by others.[34]

The elders of the landowning lineages usually controlled the most important Poro offices and made the important decisions. The Poro was responsible for the land and consulted on all land disputes. Before the Liberian government's takeover, the Poro ajudicated all murder cases, built public works projects like bridges, and even set limits on hunting game.[35] The Poro was, in short, a means through which the elders could regulate all of the economic processes central to Kpelle society. It controlled land and other natural resources and built the little infrastructure which existed.

The women's branch, the Sande, was run by women but ultimately controlled by men. It ran a school for girls to teach them the domestic skills the society deemed necessary. Anthropologist Caroline Bledsoe found that they actually learned little that was not common knowledge anyway. The induction ceremonies allowed the elders to control the number of marriageable women in the community. Women were not considered full social adults and desirable marriage partners until initiation into the Sande.[36] To the

----

34. J.D. Curran, "Sanoghie Notes," Muhlenberg Tidings 2,8 (February, 1919).

35. William Welmers, Spoken Kpelle (Liberia: Lutheran Church in Liberia, 1948)

36. See Caroline Bledsoe, Women and Marriage in Kpelle Society, pp 71-75 for a full description of the Sande's

Kpelle the Poro was not simply a tool whereby the elders could control Kpelle society. If the Kpelle had seen it as such it would not have been effective. The Poro was an effective tool for social control because of its religious and cultural importance.

Put quite simply, to be a "real Kpelle" one had to belong to the Poro Society. Poro initiation was not simply a social experience, but the major cultural experience. During initiation "Kpelleness"- the essentials of being a Kpelle- was transmitted. As foreign influences increased in importance in Sanoyea, the Poro would remain a haven for Kpelleness.

Kinship social relations, therefore, had their economic basis in agricultural production and found religious expression and ideological support in the Poro society. A second system of social relations coexisted and overlapped with the kinship system. Those individuals who became wealthy or had high status in the community were known as "big men." These "big men" were loci of economic, social and political power within Kpelle society and could attract lower status, less powerful and poorer people into mutually beneficial patron/client relationships. The patrons needed these relationships to obtain labor, warriors and political support. Clients needed protection from other powerful people, access to land and women, and, in hard times, money or food.[37] Before the Liberian government's "pacification" of the interior, patrons

----
controls over reproduction.

37. Interview with Peter Giddings, January 19, 1977.

protected their clients from kidnapping and raids by neighboring big men. Today protection is needed from the arbitrary fines and jail sentences in court cases in which social connections are often the determinant of verdicts.

Becoming a "big man" in Kpelle society depended on control over the economic resources which led to wealth and the ability to transform those resources into political power. As we shall see from an examination of Sanoyea Kpelle history, the means to do this changed over the course of time. Within the lineage system an individual became wealthy by controlling land or labor. A person usually controlled a great deal of land only if he were among the first to settle in the area. However, as long as population density remained low relative to usable land, labor rather than land, was the relatively scarce resource. For landowners, wealth therefore came to depend on the accumulation of rights to labor. One way to accumulate labor was with women so men with many wives became wealthy. The more wives a person had, the more land he could bring into production. Production surpluses could be traded or used to attract clients. The control of rights to women therefore formed a major economic resource. Bridewealth paid in cash, goods or labor brought income to those with daughters.

Once a person had accumulated some wealth other avenues to obtain labor became available to him. People tried to establish as many alliances with "big men" as possible. People gave their children to powerful well-to-do people to be raised as wards and treated as part of the family. Families tried to marry their daughters to powerful people to establish affinal linkages to important lineages.

"Big men" therefore attracted and could afford enough wives to become "wife lenders." A "big man" would allow a poorer man to take one of his wives as a consort in exchange for labor. Any children from the union belonged to the rich man. Less formal unions often resulted in adultery charges and fines which the rich used as an additional source of income. "Big men" used marriage rights to women to build a following by creating debts and alliances.[38]

The "big man" elite often coincided with the landowning elite until avenues to wealth outside the agricultural sphere became available. At various times, however, trade, connections with the Liberians on the coast, and political advancement not controlled by the landowners threatened the landowning elite's monopoly on status and privilege.

The ruling group in the Kpelle stratification system, therefore, contained those who had achieved status through wealth and those who had ascribed status as members of the original settling family. Both kinds of status showed up in the religious status system. Harley's study of the Poro revealed a complex arrangement of ritual offices reflecting the various degrees of status. Ownership of the highest offices

----

38. Caroline Bledsoe, Women and Marriage in Kpelle Society, pp. 98-99.

remained in the hands of the most important lineages and was passed down from one generation to the next. Less important offices could be purchased by other wealthy men in the community.[39] Several other secret societies, the Moling (Spirit) Society, and the Mina (Witchfinding) Society, both closely connected with the Poro, seem to have followed a similar pattern. Other societies, notably the Snake Society, appear to have been more open. Anyone with the necessary membership fees could join these societies and gradually rise to prominent positions by buying more of the society's secret medicines.

Although difficult to substantiate, it seems possible that the Poro complex of secret societies tended to preserve the ascribed status system while the achievement system found more expression in the non-Poro societies. In other words, the old guard maintained control of the Poro while the newer wealthy element could only reach the top of the non-Poro, and therefore less important, secret societies.[40] Political leadership and Poro leadership tended to coincide because the important people in the commmunity usually rose to the top in both. Whether the chief became the tool of the Poro or the Poro became the chief's tool depended upon the competition among the

----

39. George Harley, "Notes on the Poro," p. 31; Richard M. Fulton, "The Political Structure and Functions of Poro in Kpelle Society," American Anthropologist 74 (1972): 1223.

40. Richard M. Fulton, "The Political Structure and Function of Poro," pp. 1223-24.

area's important personages and the balance of power at any given time. Power- political, economic and social- tended to concentrate in the hands of a small group of people.[41]

The Liberian government's imposition of indirect rule over the various Kpelle chiefdoms in 1910-20 merely built upon this precolonial political system. Political position usually depended upon first having established one's self as a "big man" or as the head of an important landowning lineage. Before the Liberian government takeover, this region contained several small political units headed by "big men" and peopled by their relatives and clients. The Liberian government instituted a system of paramount chiefs confirming the political position of the person they felt was the most powerful in the area.[42] The paramount chiefs appointed several subchiefs to assist in their rule. During the 1920's the subchief system was changed to a clan chief system in which districts within the chiefdom selected their own local leaders who were called clan chiefs. The elders of the districts usually chose one of the local landowners or "big men" to fill this post.[43] This new hierarchy of chiefs no longer expressed the will of the elders, but that of the Liberian government. They served to

----

41. Fulton, "The Political Structure and Function of Poro," pp. 1223, 1225. Also interviews with Dougba Carranda, Peter Giddings, Moses Giddings,

42. Interview with Peter Giddings, January 19, 1977.

43. Interviews with Kekura Nyang, May 3, 1977 and Mulbah Dangolu, May 3, 1977.

collect taxes, adjudicate disputes, and transmit the Liberian government's demands to the people.

> [In the past] when the clan chief had something he wanted the clan to do, he would call the elders together and go before them. They would sit down and talk together and decide what they wanted...but these new clan chiefs all they can do when they come from Sanoyea with their big letter [government commission] is just tell us this is the thing the government wants for you people to do. They will never inform us or even ask us what we want to do.[44]

Political positions became sinecures and gave the chiefs an opportunity to increase their own wealth and clientage. Chiefs could manipulate tax revenues and collection procedures, court fines and graft to their own advantage. It was quite likely that a person was wealthy and of high status when he entered political office, but it was certain that he would be wealthier once in office.

Chapters 2 and 3 will discuss the changes which the Liberian government's takeover brings to Sanoyea in more detail. At this juncture the important point is that despite changes in the nature of political office, insofar as local support was necessary to gain office, the kinship and big man status systems continued into the colonial period. The Poro society's role in these

----

44. Interview with Kekura Gbanakao, May 3, 1977.

systems has been discussed; our next task is to consider how other aspects of Kpelle religion are related to these systems of social relations.

The landowners and the big men gained their control over economic resources from two different though overlapping systems of social relations of production. The landowners derived their control of land and labor from kinship relations and maintained it by stressing an individual's obligations to his kinship group. Group solidarity, deference to elders and membership in the Poro society all supported the privileged economic and political position of lineage elders. Although "big men" may initially have drawn their position from the lineage system, their power came to rest on patron/client relations outside the lineage system. Their position was based upon an ideology of individual achievement, boldness and initiative that often conflicted with the values emphasized in the kinship system. Although writing of a different mid-20th century village, anthropologist James Gibbs' portrait of Kpelle society comes amazingly close to Sanoyea from c.1900-1958,

> Kpelle culture has two conflicting dominant themes. The first is a stress on personal autonomy and the individual achievement of status.... Throughout there is not too subtle a stress on the instrumental manipulation of others to one's own advantage....In a society where the achievement principle is widely followed, it is clear that competitive rivalries and

shifting allegiances can be a source of considerable friction. This is especially true where, as in Kpelle society, kinship groups are weak and exercise few restraints on the individual. Those in constituted authority are constantly faced with the unsettling possibility of being replaced by the newly powerful.[45]

The key to understanding Kpelle religion is to examine how it reflects and affects the Kpelle power relationships and these ideological conflicts. During the c.1900-1958 period which I will discuss, there were pressures in Sanoyea to maintain cultural patterns and social groupings as well as opportunities and cultural approval for ambitious men who desired wealth and power. Jealousies arose, however, as the Kpelle resented those who succeeded in gaining those goals. In such a situation the supernatural became a battlefield for men's intrigues. The conflicting ideologies revealed themselves in the Kpelle religious "model of reality," that is, the way of explaining the world; in the attitudes toward manipulation of the supernatural; and in social group rituals. An examination of each of these in turn will help show how the Kpelle religion represents those social relationships most important to the Kpelle.

Belief in a Supreme Being, several kinds of lesser supernatural beings, and use of sacrifices, witchcraft, dreams, divination, and medicines form the

----

45. James Gibbs, "The Kpelle of Liberia," pp. 229-230.

framework for the Kpelle model of reality. Upon this framework the Kpelle have constructed a system of explanation which makes unusual events, illness and misfortune intelligible. Anthropologist Robin Horton has compared African religious beliefs to Western science in that both are systems of thought which locate causes in bodies of theory. By bodies of theory he means causal contexts wider than those of the common sense world. Horton realizes that the level of theory, that is, the context in which the event is placed, varies. Sometimes common sense or natural phenomena can provide an adequate explanation, but at other times a higher theoretical level- in the Kpelle case the supernatural- explains the event.[46]

The Kpelle realize that many events, for example common illnesses, have non supernatural causes. However as Evans-Pritchard pointed out, even for these common occurences the question is sometimes, "why did they occur?" rather than "how?" The man may have sprained his foot by tripping over a root, but the important question is why did he trip over it this time and not the other times he had taken this path? Why did the root trip this man and not the others who had walked by? [47]

These questions about common events can be answered by reference to supernatural agencies.

----

46. Robin Horton, "African Traditional Thought and Western Science," Africa 37 (1967):58-59.

47. E.E. Evans-Pritchard, Witchcraft Among the Azande, (London: Oxford University Press, 1937), p. 66.

Unusual events such as illnesses that arise suddenly and kill quickly or those which linger on despite all attempts to cure them, also call for explanations that go beyond the ordinary ones.

The Kpelle look for the causes of such events in the actions of people as illustrated in this 1934 incident:

> At about ten o'clock in the morning the people were all together on the market ground. As it is a custom by the natives a man is appointed to announce to the people that the market is open before anyone begins to trade. As I was told, the previous night the announcer had a dream. He dreamed that there would be no trading on the market ground the next day. When the day broke he told the dream to the people but they did not pay any attention to him. Being that it was his business to open the market, he had to perform his business.
>
> He then went to the market and as he was about to open, a large tree on the market yard cracked, but they did not pay any attention to the cracking of the tree. After a few minutes the tree cracked more and came down with force and fell on the ground. When the tree fell eighteen people were killed on the spot and thirty were badly wounded...
>
> There is a rule among the native people that a market place must always be below the town

and never above the town. Sometime before this accident the people had carried the market place above the town. The chief objected but they did not listen. The Chief then forbade any of his family to attend the market so that when the accident occurred none of his family people were hurt.

Before the accident a handkerchief had been missing from a Mandingo trader who came to this town. This man asked the Announcer of the town to make an announcement about his handkerchief. The announcement was made but the handkerchief could not be found. Then he told the people that since his handkerchief cannot be found, the people of the town will suffer for it in some way....I was told he hid some medicine under the tree which caused the accident.[48]

This story contains multiple causes for the tragedy and instructs people in how to behave to avoid such accidents. Note that the storyteller has not suggested that the event was coincidence or just plain bad luck. No impersonal or capricious forces acted, no spirits or supernatural beings punished men for sins even though human culpability forms part of the explanation. The people refused to heed the dream warning, they had breached custom by building the market above the town, and they had disobeyed their chief. The Muslim trader,

----

48. October 10, 1934, Moses Washington to W.A. Moser, Sanoyea Mission Records.

an outsider with supernatural powers, had used medicine to cause the accident even though he had received hospitable treatment. The morals of the story are clear; people must pay attention to dreams, to customs and to their leaders because the world contains evil people who can cause misfortune. These morals support the existing power structure by urging deference to established authority.

The Kpelle couch their religious explanations in terms of human action and human interaction with the supernatural world. The essential element of Kpelle religious explanation is that morality lies not in their gods but in themselves. The supernatural universe is morally neutral, but both good and evil men can manipulate it. If the Kpelle world contains a very pessimistic, though sometimes realistic, picture of their fellow man, it also contains the optimistic view that man can, through his actions, change his state of affairs. In Kpelle religion clever men could manipulate the supernatural to achieve success while evil men manipulated it to harm the community.

The Kpelle hold an ambivalent attitude toward successful manipulation of the supernatural. They approve of some manipulations, for example ancestor veneration, while they disapprove of others- especially those which resulted in illness or death- unless used on behalf of the community. To put it more accurately, jealousies and social disapproval are expressed through accusations of the use of socially disapproved supernatural measures while social approbation is expressed in tales of successful supernatural manipulations.

This understanding of the Sanoyea Kpelle world view and its social context helps explain their religious behavior and ritual. The Kpelle model "for" reality, the plan for living in the common sense world, calls for the manipulation of the supernatural both to get what one wants out of life and to protect against the supernatural attacks of others. Kpelle ritual usually takes the form of sacrifice to a supernatural being in order to get aid or in the use of Kpelle medicines. "Sale," the Kpelle word for medicine, is a generic term for any substance or procedure with which someone can effect events in the natural world.

The best way to understand the Kpelle models of and for reality is to trace the process for dealing with misfortune from the diagnostic techniques to possible supernatural causes and the options for action. Since the Kpelle model of reality provides several possible causes for misfortune, a Kpelle person must first discover the source of his problem if he is to take appropriate action. As the story of the accident in the market suggests, breaches of custom or social regulations can lead to misfortune. Conscious and unconscious human interaction with spirits and the very human motives of the spirits themselves also serve to explain unfortunate events. The Kpelle usually use dreams, divination and the intuition of medical practitioners to diagnose causes.

The importance of dreams in Kpelle religion cannot be overemphasized. As one man said, "People here...believe in dreams more than anything else...they know that dreams are reality.[49] Dreams are a form of communication between the natural and supernatural worlds. Dreams foretell disaster, indicate the cause of illness and also provide cures. Dreams can bring knowledge of sacrificial obligations which have not been met and of jealous people who may have instigated supernatural actions.

Divination among the Kpelle involves kola nuts. At sacrifices people address questions to the spirits, then toss split kola nuts to determine the spirit's response. The spirit's answer depends on the position of the kola nuts when they landed. People were not averse to making changes if things did not work out right.

> The kola nut is supposed to be cast with two hands [speaker indicates short underhand motion with both hands in front of the body] but in my casting of the kola I would move one hand from there and cast it with one hand. So, the two split sides couldn't come up. This means that there was no agreement [from the spirit] no harmony whatsoever. So they would move me from there quick and take my sister.[50]

Muslims introduced a new kind of divination called "sand playing." There were different forms of sand playing, that practiced by literate Muslims, and

----

49. Interview with Moses Giddings, May 28, 1977.
50. Interview with Edward Gouto, October 27, 1976.

those practiced by people who could not read. The literate form involve writing the names of the great prophets, Abraham, Moses, Jesus and Muhammad, then counting pebbles according to a formula. If the count ended on Moses's name, for example, the sand player based his diagnosis, prediction or advice on some event that had happened in the appropriate year of Moses's life.[51] The non-literate divinations consist either of drawing geomantic figures with sand or manipulating vials of colored sand. The non-literate forms probably called for trance and a bit of showmanship as the following description, written by a missionary, shows,

> on the floor is...[an animal] skin; generously sprinkled with small bottles of colored sand, small pouches containing other secret medicines and more miscellaneous charms. The fortune teller [sand player] sits cross-legged on the floor facing this mass of gadgetry and puts on a mask made of monkey skin and imposingly decorated with supposedly hideous designs, and from which a number of small brass bells and other noisemakers are suspended. Before telling a fortune, he sings at a tremendous rate of speed in falsetto, shaking his head from side to side all the time, at a rate which would give most people a bad headache. After several minutes of this, he rearranges the bottles and charms in front of him,

----

51. Interview with Muluba Keita, May 31, 1977.

scrutinizes several of them carefully, probably shakes some of them up, and then tells the future.[52]

After the establishment of a Muslim community in 1916, these Muslim forms of divination came to be the most commonly used in Sanoyea.

Once someone has determined the cause of an illness, one can either offer the sacrifice to the proper spirit or obtain medicine to ward off or correct the condition. Unlike Westerners, the Kpelle would not appeal directly to the Supreme Being. God, the creator of the world and an immanent force underlying all other religious beliefs, presides over the Kpelle cosmology. As the Kpelle express it, "God's name is always there" whenever they perform a ritual. Nevertheless, the Kpelle had no rituals specifically directed to the high God although direct entreaty in times of desperation did occur.[53] This lack of communication parallels other practices in Kpelle society. Important chiefs and Poro personages also were never approached directly but only through interpreters or "speakers."

Everything - animals, plants, rocks, mountains and bodies of water - has its spirit in Kpelle religion. The Kpelle in effect enter into patron/client relationships with the spirit world and

----

52. William Welmers, "Secret Medicines, Magic and Rites of the Kpelle Tribe of Liberia," Southwestern Journal of Anthropology 5 (1949): 219.

53. Interview with Amanda Gardiner, March 3, 1977.

treat these spirits like other patrons in Kpelle society. They feel that their patrons should represent, protect and argue on their behalf with the higher authorities. The Kpelle addressed communication to God through these intermediaries.

> We used to serve...the plantain banana, trees, rocks, water. We used to go there to pray to them. They used to cook rice and carry it there, then take the kola and throw it down.... They say, "God help us so that we can win the war," or "God help us so that this person who is sick can get well."...Before we do this we must say "God,"...God's name was always the first.[54]

Individuals often maintained a plant, commonly a banana plant, to use as a familiar.

> When a man becomes of age he must go and give his totem his respect. On a good morning, never at any other time of the day, he and his wife go out to the spot where they intend to plant the banana. The usual kind is the long plantain-like banana. After the planting, they make their sacrifice, which is either a white or red chicken...Then they pray, "O banana, you are behind us. You are given to us from God. You are to watch over us. This chicken we put under you. You must watch and guard us now, and keep us.

----

54. Interview with Bakweli Zentei, March 22, 1977.

> As the bananas are usually planted outside the town, and the chicken cannot be left there under the plant, and as it will run around anyway and not stay, a piece of cotton is placed under the plant in case the chicken is white and a colanut is used if the chicken is red....The chicken is not taken back into town and becomes like the banana, a tabu, i.e. it cannot be eaten and is at the same time a powerful medicine.[55]

Some nature spirits appear in dreams to form sexual liaisons with people. In exchange for sexual fidelity to the spirit, that is, continence in the natural world, the spirit would grant various favors and good fortune.[56] Still other nature spirits are not associated with any particular entity and lived in the deep forests much like the hobgoblins in Western folklore.[57]

Birth spirits form a special category of nature spirits. The spirit of a plant or an animal may possess a person at birth. That person will grow to have the physical characteristics of the birth spirit. For example, a strong man might be said to have a leopard or an elephant as his birth spirit and must

----

55. H.O. Rohde, "The Banana Cult," Muhlenberg Tidings 1,9 (April,1916), Lutheran Church in Liberia Archive.

56. Interview with Edward Gouto, October 27, 1976.

57. William Welmers, Spoken Kpelle (Liberia: Lutheran Church in Liberia, 1948), Unit 27, p. 6.

avoid eating that meat.[58] Some people can change into their birth spirits, so hunters must be careful not to shoot certain animals. Injury caused to a person in animal form will appear when the person regains human form. Consequently, some human illnesses are attributed to one's birth spirit's activities.[59] One informant remembered a woman who had the ability to change into her elephant birth spirit. Her brother, a hunter, would lie in wait while she led a herd of elephants to him. He would take care not to shoot the lead elephant, his sister, but could kill one of the others.[60]

The ancestors form a separate and important category of spirits. One's ancestors have a great deal of influence over their descendants. The Kpelle view their ancestors as the repository of Kpelle wisdom, as advocates for their descendants in communications with God, and as spiritual arbiters for proper kinship relations. Infertility, for example, is a concern not only of the community but of the ancestors as well, for the ancestors are concerned with the continuation of their line. If a woman were barren a ritual would ask that the ancestor speak to God on his or her descendant's behalf.[61] If people suspected that improper behavior toward relatives or failure to

----

58. William Welmers, Spoken Kpelle, Unit 26, pp. 2-3.

59. Interview with Amanda Gardiner, March 3, 1977.

60. Interview with Kekura Gbanakao, April 24, 1977.

61. Interview with Amanda Gardiner March 3, 1977.

perform the proper ancestor rituals had caused the infertility, the ritual would ask for forgiveness.

The Kpelle try to stay in contact with the dead through personal objects that once belonged to the departed.

> When they carry the body to the grave they will take the thing that the person always had with them, either a knife, a bracelet or ring or beads...they would take it off, dip it in some ashes...and rub it on the person's heart. That is for the person's spirit to enter into [it]. They would take it and lay it aside, then they would bury the body....They would place [the object] in a plate and set it behind the door. Every new moon they would make sacrifice to it. They would cook rice, kill chicken and cook, have a big feast and carry some to the grave and throw it there. And then they would throw some all around the town...they are feeding the ancestor spirit.[62]

These periodic rituals, called "ngamua kweni," held great importance for the Kpelle. As one man exressed it,

> the idea was to relate me to our ancestors, my great,great,great, great grandparents who lived before. The idea was that although

----

62. Interview with Amanda Gardiner, March 3, 1977.

> they were dead they were still part of me, in
> the spiritual world we are still linked and I
> must do something to please them.[63]

It was also important to stay on the good side of the spirits of the dead because they were potentially dangerous beings who could do one harm. The ancestor shades could bring on misfortune even without entering into transactions with the living. The Kpelle believe that the dead have the same feelings and emotions they had when alive but they have become much more powerful. Vengeful spirits might return to attack those who have harmed them while alive. Even sighting a spirit was thought to be dangerous so that such returns threatened the entire community.[64] At Kpelle funerals the eldest member of the deceased's family usually addressed the corpse to try to mend any grudges the departed might have with the living.

> All the family would gather around and say
> whatever they wanted to say to the
> dead.....They would say, "Well...when you
> were here we lived peaceably here together.
> I didn't do any big bad thing to you, neither
> did you to me. Now while you have gone to
> the true side... now while you are in
> heaven, please don't frown at me.[65]

----

63. Interview with Bishop Roland Payne, October 22, 1976.

64. William Welmers, <u>Spoken Kpelle</u>, Unit 27, p. 6.

65. Interview with Amanda Gardiner, March 3, 1977.

Note that even when spirits act on their own volition without human instigation it is because they are displaying human characteristics and reflecting the Kpelle view of human nature.

Although the ancestors are potentially harmful I could not find any examples of their manipulation to harm others. All examples of such manipulation, that is, witchcraft, involved the nature spirits, birth spirits or two other types of supernatural beings: the dream spirits and the water people. A dream spirit is a manifestation of a person's soul and everyone has one. The souls of certain individuals move about causing mischief while the person sleeps. The mischief may be petty, destroying rice or stealing livestock, or it may be more serious, causing illness especially in children.[66] The evidence that one's dream soul has caused harm is that the person has dreamed of eating meat. Although the individual might be unaware of his dream spirit's activities, people still hold him responsible for any illness or misfortune that is traced back to it.[67]

The water people are beings quite similar to humans who live in the creeks and rivers which run throughout Kpelle country. Water people replicate human society in their underwater villages and towns.[68] The water people are also mischief makers

----

66. Interview with Nee Kani, July 11, 1977.
67. James Gibbs, "The Kpelle of Liberia, " p. 228.
68. William Welmers Spoken Kpelle, Unit 31, p. 4.

and if there were no other apparent causes they were held responsible for misfortunes which occur near or on the water. They are said to overturn boats, wash away bridges and even to drown people.[69] Humans can make agreements with the water people to exchange a young relative for aid in gaining power or position. A child who has been "sold in the water", as the Kpelle say, will fall ill and eventually die.[70]

The dream spirits and the transactions between humans, water people and nature spirits constitute different kinds of witchcraft. The dream spirits are an unintended or unconscious form of witchcraft which reflects the hidden desires and unspoken feelings- usually jealousies- which the Kpelle feel abound in village life. The person who consciously arranges to injure others is a person who poses even greater dangers to the community. The motives behind such actions - therefore the greater threats to the community - are not only jealousy but also revenge and ambition.

The most common targets for witchcraft are infants and important people. The Kpelle believe that babies are the most likely victims of witchcraft because they are the most vulnerable.[71] The high incidence of infant mortality and importance of

----

69. Interviews with Amanda Gardiner, March 3, 1977 and Nee Kani, July 11, 1977.

70. Interview with Edward Gouto, October 27, 1976.

71. Interview with Amanda Gardiner, March 11, 1977.

children explain the prevalance of these beliefs. Everyone wants many healthy and beautiful children and those who did not have them are deemed to be jealous of those who did.[72] Those who want to achieve their ambitions are deemed willing to forfeit a child of their family, something valuable as well as vulnerable.

Paradoxically "big men" are most often believed to be both the users of witchcraft and the victims of witchcraft. Someone who has advanced too quickly or outside the lineage system is often thought to have used witchcraft. Younger people who had gained political office are often accused of having sold a relative to the water people in order to achieve it. Witchcraft was also one of the few ways powerless people could affect the powerful and gain revenge for mistreatment. One informant explained that he was not sure witchcraft existed but he had noticed that "big men" tended to die younger.[73]

Regardless of whether dream spirits actually go abroad at night or whether water people live in the creeks, witchcraft is a very real occurrence among the Kpelle because the Kpelle behave as if these events do happen. A person who dreams of eating meat accepts his guilt if someone else falls ill and then searches for a possible motive or any ill feelings he might have held

----

72. Interview with Amanda Gardiner, March 11, 1977.
73. Interview with Alexander Mulbah, April 29, 1977.

toward that person.[74]

Some people do go to medical practitioners to arrange transactions with the water people, but people more commonly attribute such actions to others. Witchcraft accusations represent real tensions in Kpelle society and reflect the Kpelle view of human nature.

Witchcraft accusations were common in Sanoyea during the 1920-56 period. Anthropologist Mary Douglas argues that witchcraft becomes the major religious idiom in any society where the goals the society presents to individuals are contradictory or ambiguous and the society puts great pressure upon its members to live up to its norms.[75]

As we shall see in the next chapter there were great pressures upon people in Sanoyea to maintain cultural patterns and social groupings as well as opportunities and cultural approval for ambitious men who desired wealth and power. The conservative ideologies and values of the kinship social structure and the individualism of the "big men" system often conflicted. Witchcraft accusations were another manifestation of this conflict.

Kpelle medicines offer another way to manipulate events in the real world. Some of the medical

----

74. Pauline Ziegler, "So Much They Need to Change," Foreign Missionary 70,6 (June, 1950): 29-30.

75. Mary Douglas, Natural Symbols, (N.Y.: Random House, Vintage Books edition, 1970) pp. 87-88.

practices are quite akin to Western techniques- the use of herbal pharmacology, the isolation of contagious diseased patients, and rather advanced bonesetting procedures which included bone grafts with animal bones.[76] Other medicines ("sale") are more akin to what has been called sympathetic magic. With these medicines the procedure for preparing them "acts out" the effects the medicines are supposed to have. One medicine which is supposed to prevent a person from doing something is made by using that person's hair, fingernails or just his name. The practitioner immobilizes the victim by placing the medicine in the ground or in the water.[77]

The Kpelle, just like Westerners, first try their own "medicine cabinets" when an illness strikes.[78] Certain common medicines are known and used by all. Some people, particularly elderly women, know a few medicines beyond the common ones and they are called upon whenever their specialty is needed. A person who knows several medicines or who belongs to one of the secret societies is called a "zo."[79] These medical practitioners learn their medicines either through dreams, intuition, or by purchasing that knowledge from others.

----

76. William Welmers, "Secret Medicines," p. 213.
77. William Welmers, "Secret Medicines," p. 216.
78. William Welmers, "Secret Medicines," p. 211.
79. William Welmers, "Secret Medicines," p. 211.

> I bought many [medicines] from other people. That's how I got most of them. Yes, when I see anybody cure anybody, then I will buy the medicine...sometimes my mind would just lead me. I would see a sickness and then my mind would lead me to a certain leaf. And I would go and stand there and look at it. I mean it would just be like someone is whispering something to me, but it wasn't like that. It would just come to my mind what to do. That's why people say I was a born herbist.[80]

The knowledge of medicines is a precious commodity in Kpelle society. Certain secret societies own the medicine to cure specific ailments and a person has to join the society in order to learn the treatment. After paying one's dues in the Snake Society for example (the Kpelle would call this purchasing the "head of the society") one learns the treatment for snakebites. one could then earn money by treating snakebite victims.[81]

Medicines therefore offer an opportunity to manipulate the supernatural world just as the sacrificial rituals do. Moreover, medicines offer an avenue for entrepreneurs to supplement their income and to gain prestige outside of the normal channels. Medicine men and other religious practicioners did not

----

80. Interview with Amanda Gardiner, March 3, 1977.
81. William Welmers, "Secret Medicines," p. 211.

make enough to support themselves and had to farm to augment their incomes.[82] However, their knowledge did allow them to gain privileges and rank within Kpelle society. Medicines too could be used for both good and evil purposes, to launch supernatural attacks against others and to protect oneself against such attacks. In their search for new ways to control the supernatural, the Kpelle eagerly sought out new medicines. This made the acceptance of Western and Muslim medicines quite easy.

In tracing the Kpelle religious system from divination to medicine, that is from diagnosis to cure, it has become clear that religion gives concrete form to the tensions of Kpelle social relations. The Kpelle respond to these tensions not only as individuals but also as members of groups. The corporate groups important to Kpelle society- the household, the extended family, the town ward or quarter and the town or village- all have rituals to perform as a group. These rituals integrate corporate groups by creating networks of religious obligations parallel to the kinship labor obligations. It is within these groups that we see the "stress on conformity and regulation."[83]

Kpelle households usually consist of a nuclear family with only one or two additions, usually a man's mother or brother. Household members became involved

----

82. Interviews with Amanda Gardiner, March 3, 1977 and Alexander Mulbah, April 29, 1977.

83. James Gibbs, "The Kpelle of Liberia," p. 230.

in each individual's personal sacrifices. The sacrifices to a personal plant familiar which I have mentioned above were important household projects with wives and children participating. When a man had a child, he often planted a banana so the child could conduct his own sacrifices as he grew older.[84] Religious beliefs were thus passed down within the household and each household member felt an obligation to participate.

For the most part the Kpelle trace their ancestry through the father, but ritual positions reside with the father's sister's son or daughter, the "maa le nuu." Whenever extended families did cooperate to perform sacrifices for their ancestors, the ngamua rituals, the "maa le nuu" performed the sacrifice.[85] Despite the weakness of patrilineages as corporate groups, the ngamua ceremonies were quite important in Sanoyea. Quite possibly the rituals became more important in Sanoyea because other methods to maintain the extended family were weaker.

The well-being of some patrilineages intertwine with the well-being of certain species of plants or animals. Members of these families could not eat such animals or plants and these food taboos acted like totems to identify kinsmen no matter how distant. People in Sanoyea sometimes define their relationships to people in terms of their food taboos even when these

----

84. Interview with Charles Wellington, April 21, 1977.

85. Interview with Benda Gwiningali, April 26, 1977.

people lived elsewhere.[86] These food taboos therefore create a rather loose kinship network that extended to other parts of Kpelleland.

Ancestors are the most important spiritual beings for the patrilineages. Ideas about the ancestors closely correspond to ideas about life after death. The Kpelle believe that the dead go to "God's town" or the "ancestor's town" located across a wide river or at the top of a steep hill.[87] Admission to God's town does not depend upon proper conduct as it does in Christian belief, so that all shades go there.[88]

Beryl Bellman, working in a northeastern Kpelle chiefdom far from Sanoyea, found that those Kpelle considered God's town a replication of the ideal pattern for a Kpelle town. Patrilineages lived together within the town so that family structure and town arrangement coincided.[89] I found no evidence to suggest that the Sanoyea Kpelle held this belief, perhaps because of the weaker patrilineages. The Sanoyea Kpelle did show a great desire to rejoin their ancestors when they died. The mission taught belief that only Christians entered heaven pressured converts to have their relatives baptized as well in order to

----

86. Interview with Benda Gwiningali, April 26, 1977.

87. H.O. Rohde, "Death in the Kpelle Mind," Muhlenberg Tidings 1,11 (June, 1916): 2.

88. William Welmers, Spoken Kpelle, Unit 3. pp. 2-3.

89. Beryl Bellman, Village of Curers and Assassins, (The Hague: Mouton,), pp. 129-130.

reunite the family after death.[90]

Larger Kpelle towns contain subsections built around the settlements of important families. Although ostensibly built around patrilineages, these town wards or "quarters" are little more than neighborhoods. Quarter chiefs are the acknowledged local religious leaders and performed sacrifices for the welfare of the quarter. The quarter system allowed immigrants like the Muslims to maintain their own cultural and religious identity while becoming part of the town.

Townspeople could also take action as a group to promote the general welfare and to prevent epidemics or other natural catastrophes. Many towns had a town medicine, a bundle of different objects, kept at the town's entrance to keep away evil spirits.[91] The town's founding family performed periodic sacrifices and led any rite performed by the town as a whole. When disease threatened the town, all members had to contribute to a cleansing ritual. Each household provided fagots for a fire burned outside the town, which cleansed the town of the disease.[92] When war parties prepared to fight, the entire town held sacrifices to insure their success and safety. The town chief usually organized and led these activities thus recognizing and emphasizing his authority.

----

90. Interview with Nee Pee, March 18, 1977.
91. William Welmers, "Secret Medicines," p. 214.
92. Interview with Amanda Gardiner, March 3, 1977.

The Kpelle group rituals therefore both reflected and reinforced Kpelle social and political divisions. Religious duties were associated with political office and position of authority. The deference shown each leader mirrored his or her importance in Kpelle social, political and economic relationships.

To understand a religious system one must go beyond simply looking at the correlation between religious beliefs and social structure. One must understand that the two act upon each other as well as reflect each other. I have looked not only at the correlations between religion and social structure but also at how the religious system colors the way the Kpelle see social relationships. I have argued that the conflict between the stress on individual achievement and the mixture of resentment and respect for those who succeed has produced a manipulative model of reality. The Kpelle explanatory system, however, not only reflects the tensions and antagonisms of Kpelle village life, it provides an arena in which those tensions can be acted upon. The existence of such an arena not only intensifies the mistrust that forms part of the Kpelle world view, it also provides security by giving one the means to combat one's antagonists.

The Kpelle world view also generates religious focal points around which social groups gather. The Kpelle feel that they face threats as members of social groups as well as individuals. The religious rituals for group protection provide an integrative force to balance the cultural stress on individual achievement that Gibbs has pointed out. Finally, at the widest level of group integration, the Poro Society, we find not just another social group but a cultural group which maintained and transmitted the traditions, knowledge and essence of Kpelle culture.

In order to understand Sanoyea religious change one must look at the religious system in its historical context. In this chapter I have simply introduced those relationships between society and religion which dominate the c.1900-1958 period. In the next chapter I will show how these relationships have developed out of particular historical circumstances. I will argue that the period between 1920 and 1958 saw Sanoyea's growing involvement with the Americo Liberian world. As the Kpelle became a colonized people more fully exposed to Americo Liberian influences, their religion continued to express the conflicts between the Kpelle achievement ethic, the social pressures toward conformity and the maintenance of Kpelle cultural distinctiveness. The 1912 arrival of the Liberian government in Sanoyea intensified political intrigue, opened new, though limited opportunities for wealth and power, and worsened economic conditions for most Kpelle. These developments exacerbated the tensions in Kpelle society.

CHAPTER TWO

Sanoyea and the "Kwi" World c.1874-1920

In the last chapter I have shown how political power, wealth and status in Kpelle society depend upon turning political or economic position into patron client relationships. The political history of Sanoyea is a history of changes in the sources of political power. One family - the Giddings family - managed to maintain control of Sanoyea from around 1874 to 1956 and to expand Sanoyea from a single small settlement to an important chiefdom. Each successive ruler had to adapt to the growing intrusion of the Americo Liberian state and its foreign culture. The Sanoyea leadership's political decisions ultimately led to the establishment of the Lutheran mission in Sanoyea and changes in the townspeople's religious behavior.

I will argue that the strengthening of the ties between the Americo Liberians and the Sanoyea leaders not only introduced a new religion, but also strengthened several aspects of the indigenous religion. Because of the relationship between religion and leadership in Kpelle society, the Kpelle rulers had to translate political power they gained by contact with the Americo Liberian colonizers into power within Kpelle religious institutions. The confrontation with the culture of the Americo Liberians - called the "kwi" culture by the Kpelle - led to a reaffirmation of Kpelle cultural values.

In this chapter I will trace the separate histories of the Sanoyea Kpelle, the Americo Liberians and the Lutheran missionaries to see how they came to confront each other in Sanoyea by 1920. The next chapter will examine the history of Sanoyea from the beginning of colonial rule in 1920 until 1958 when Giddings family rule effectively ended. I will show how the social forces set in motion by these groups provided an impetus for religious change and also set limits on the direction and nature of such change.

Although historians know little about early Kpelle history, one can discern several processes which help us to understand later events. The Kpelle belong to one of the later waves of Mande speaking immigrants into Liberia who pressed the earlier inhabitants into close proximity along the coast.[1] As early as the late sixteenth century, Portuguese sailors on the coast received reports of a people living in the area the Kpelle now inhabit. Rodney identifies them as the Kpelle and uses the reports to establish that the people in the interior of what is now Liberia had dominated and interfered in the affairs of the coastal people at an early date.[2]

Aside from these vague reports little is known about the Kpelle in the 17th and 18th centuries. Kpelle oral traditions tell of their dispersal from one

----

1. Warren d'Azevedo, "A Tribal Reaction to Nationalism, (part 1)" Liberian Studies Journal, 1, 1 (1969):5.

2. Walter Rodney, A History of the Upper Guinea Coast, (New York: Monthly Review Press, 1970), p. 50.

town in northern Liberia before 1600.[3]

There was a general movement northwestward across the St. Paul River then southwestward along the river toward the coast. By the late 18th or early 19th centuries they had reached their southwesternmost expansion in present day Todi and Fuama chiefdoms. Their advance was stopped there by the similarly expanding Gola speakers.[4]

The Mande immigrants were primarily farmers, but trade also became an important economic activity. At first trade was oriented towards the kingdoms of the savannah and plateaus of the interior. The Mande groups became middlemen trading coastal and forest products like salt, kola and palm oil into the interior. The arrival of the Europeans altered the trade patterns somewhat. Coastal people like the De and the Vai became the principal middlemen in a new trade between the coast and the interior - the slave trade.[5] As the slave trade expanded in the 18th century, the Gola- the people of the hinterland immediately behind the Vai- scrambled to control the trade routes to the interior. Muslim Mandinka traders came to live along the trade route in this area of

----

3. Bai T. Moore, Tribes of the Western Province and Denwoin People, (Monrovia: Department of the Interior, Republic of Liberia, 1955), p. 34

4. Warren D'Azevedo, "Tribal Reaction to Nationalism, (part 1)" p. 12.

5. See Walter Rodney, A History of the Upper Guinea Coast, for a detailed account of the slave trade in this area.

Liberia as part of a trading diaspora. Small Gola chiefdoms formed coalitions to control trade and to protect themselves from their competitors. The most important coalition centered on the town of Bopolu- north of the St. Paul river- through which passed the major trade route.[6]

The area which is now Sanoyea appears centrally located among the Kpelle chiefdoms. During the 17th and 18th centuries it was a backwater - just far enough away from all the major events and groups to be relatively peaceful, yet close enough to be affected. It was not close enough to the Bopolu trade route to become a major trade center; it was too far from the coast to participate directly in the coastal trade; and it was far enough way from the larger states in the Kpelle heartland - Gbalein, Zota, and Johkwele - to escape their control. Sanoyea became a haven for people fleeing the wars and turmoil which the slave trade, internecine disputes and economic competition had stirred up.[7]

The migrations showed the pattern common to this region and which continued on into the 20th century.

----

6. Warren D'Azevedo, "Tribal Reaction to Nationalism, (part 1)"

7. This composite picture of migrations is based upon information in several of my interviews: Benjamin Barclay, April 5, 1977, Mulbah Dangolu, May 3, 1977, Bangali Donso, May 26, 1977, Mulbah Gbamokweli, April 5, 1977, Kekura Gbanakao, April 24, 1977 and Kekura Nyang, May 3, 1977; and the model in Richard Fulton, "The Kpelle Traditional Political System," Liberian Studies Journal, 1,1 (1968): 1-19.

People in small groups migrated short distances, settled for a while in one spot, then moved on. These migrants would usually go to a settled area and ask the local leader for land to farm. People with special skills- blacksmiths or hunters for example- would attach themselves as clients to the important leaders. Once a band of migrants had settled in an area other members of that family would hear about the new settlement and come to join them. The migrants would intermarry with the local people so that the new settlement would increase in size. The settlement might branch out as members of the town moved off to start their own hamlets or "half towns" as they are called in Liberia. These "half towns" kept close ties with the main village so that the ruling family could end up controlling an area considerably larger than the original village.

The first members of the Giddings family to enter the Sanoyea area came as traders of small goods. A man named Toosolung and his two older brothers came to Sanoyea from what is now Guinea. Toosolung soon formed an adulterous liaison with one of the chief's wives which resulted in her pregnancy. When the child was born Toosolung's culpability was revealed and he and his brothers were forced to pay a large fine to the chief. Toosolung married the woman and acknowledged the child. His brothers, angered by his behavior and its cost, left the area to go to neighboring Kpelle chiefdoms. Toosolung stayed in Sanoyea and prospered as a trader.[8]

----

8. Interview with Peter Gidding, January 19, 1977.

The story of Toosolung illusrates the importance of relationships with women even in the earliest periods of Kpelle history. As I have shown, control over women's labor and reproductive capacities is an important economic resource in Kpelle society. Chiefs often used women to bind important outsiders to themselves and to acquire wealth through bridewealth payments and adultery fines. Toosolung's fine was both punitive and compensatory to make up for the loss of the woman's labor and uxorial services. Once the payment had been made Toosolung had not only gained a wife, he had also established a tie with the community.

The date of Toosolung's arrival is a matter of conjecture. His descendents claim that he arrived in the 17th century. This would place Toosolung in the first wave of Kpelle migration away from their legendary dispersal point Wyeta. Although this is possible, I found no corroborating evidence for the presence of any member of the lineage until the emergence of Toosolung's grandson, Siwi in the mid 19th century. Although the short generational spacing between Toosoloung and Siwi could be the result of lineage "telescoping," it seems unlikely that the population of the area would have been dense enough to attract merchants during the 17th century. Other informants place the arrival of these ancestors of the Giddings family at a more recent date.[9] The argument over the date of arrival has local importance because it affects the Giddings' claim to be the founding

----

9. Interview with Benjamin Barclay, April 5, 1977.

lineage or "owners of the land." As we have seen in Chapter 1 this is an important position in Kpelle politics and challenges to the Giddings family are couched in these terms. Such disputes make it difficult to establish chronologies solely based on oral traditions.

I believe that the Giddings lineage has not been telescoped and Toosolung and his brothers probably arrived in the late 18th or early 19th centuries. Most of my other accounts show that many people in the older Kpelle areas fled to the Sanoyea area to escape the wars. The increasing demand for slaves on the coast and the influx of firearms into the interior fueled these wars. This growth of the population may have attracted traders like Toosolung.

By the mid-19th century Sanoyea was no longer the peaceful haven it had once been. A Liberian explorer, Benjamin K. Anderson, passed through the region in 1874 while trying to find an alternate interior trade route in order to bypass Bopolu. His account revealed that population had become relatively dense, settlements were located close together and the disputes between villages had become much more common. Anderson found the area wracked by what he called "petty wars."[10]

Most of these wars resulted from the lack of a centralized authority to settle economic disputes. By far the most common causes of war given by my

----

10. Benjamin K. Anderson, Narrative of the Expedition Dispatched to Musahdu by the Liberian Government in 1874 (London: Frank Cass Ltd., 1971) p. 40.

informants were disputes over debts and women. In the most common cases a woman would run off with a man from another village and the man would refuse to return her or pay bridewealth for her. In other instances men from a village would kidnap a woman either for themselves or to sell to someone else.[11] The second most common cause was the failure to pay a debt to someone in another village. A person would organize a raid on the other village in order to get property or captives to satisfy the debt.

Other disputes involved rights to economically valuable territory. One such dispute involved an elephant that had been shot in one group's territory but that had died in another's. Another involved fishing rights in a pond in one village's territory which had been discovered by a man from another village.[12] Although there was certainly trade in the area, I could find no traces of rights to trade or control of trading routes as causes of war. This sharply contrasts with the situation in Gola territory across the St. Paul River ́through which the important Bopolu trade route ran.[13]

The chaos and turmoil of war had reached the Sanoyea area and it affected daily life for most people. Bands of non-Kpelle mercenaries roamed the area working for important local leaders. War had

----

11. Interview with Benjamin Barclay, April 5, 1977.

12. Interview with Mulbah Dangolu, May 3, 1977.

13. See Warren D'Azevedo, "Tribal Reaction to Nationalism, (part 1)"

become so common in the area that towns were now built with defense as a major priority. Sanoyea town, for example, was built on a hill, surrounded by a palisade, and a had a system of watchmen with torches for warning the town at the first sight of intruders.[14] "Wars" could range from small raids to major incursions which would destroy a village. Attacking warriors would kill or drive away all the men in a village while offering the women and sometimes children a choice of life or death:

> If you are a fine young boy the war chief will ask, "Would you like to be with me or do you want me to kill you?"....When the war is getting ready to finish, [the boy] will go to the chief's farm. Whenever they catch a fine woman they will ask the same question...the war chief will also get her on his farm either to become his wife or to become his servant...If they had agreed to be killed then our clan would be an empty land because there would have been no one.[15]

Although a desire to obtain slaves was not listed as one of the causes of war, war captives constituted the major source of slaves.[16] Other captives either became domestic slaves or were sold to slave traders.

----

14. Interview with Sackie Nangbora, March 16, 1977.
15. Interview with Flumo Gbodai, March 22, 1977.
16. Interview with Peter Giddings, January 19, 1977.

Within this tumultuous context Siwi Wockpaling, Toosolung's grandson, emerged as the major leader in the Sanoyea region. Siwi was at first simply the head of his lineage and the leader of the small area his family inhabited. Sometime after the middle of the 19th century Siwi and two other nearby lineage heads formed a mutual defense pact. Siwi took command as war leader whenever they were threatened by attack and he directed the military operations of all three areas. He instituted a conscription program which made death the penalty for young men and their fathers who refused to go to war.[17] This defense program was neither as revolutionary nor as influential as that of Shaka the Zulu king and military genius, but within the Liberian context it enabled the three areas to mobilize manpower and withstand their enemies.

The other areas of the confederation had at first only delegated military powers to Siwi. Informants from these areas insisted that their ancestors had been Siwi's allies not his subjects.[18] Siwi had expanded his position as a lineage leader by becoming the war leader. He used his position as a war leader to attract clients and to participate in the slave trade. He traded war captives to Vai traders from the coast who would use them as domestic slaves or sell them to neighboring African groups.[19] People who had heard about Siwi came to Sanoyea to become Siwi's clients or

----

17. Interview with Peter Giddings January 19, 1977.
18. Interview with Benjamin Barclay, April 5, 1977.
19. Interview with Peter Giddings, January 27, 1977.

simply to settle in a relatively protected area. When a Kpelle mercenary named Yakpalo Pay needed an employer, he offered his warrior band to Siwi.[20] Most informants agree that Pay greatly contributed to Siwi's military success.[21] Siwi and Pay conquered neighboring chiefdoms, forced them to pay tribute and acknowledge Siwi's overlordship. Pay would later break with Siwi and lead much of the Kpelle opposition to the Liberian government's "pacification" campaigns.[22]

By the time Siwi died, about 1911, he had become a "big man," a patron who controlled wealth and political power. Under him Sanoyea approached Richard Fulton's model of a prototypical Kpelle state.[23] In this model the ruler (loi kalong) belonged to the core lineage known as the "rulers of the land." This ruler settled land questions, marital disputes that had become public and other disputes between villages in

----

20. Interview with Peter Giddings, June 23, 1977.

21. Interview with Benjamin Barclay , April 5, 1977.

22. Several letters in the Liberian National Archive (hereafter abbreviated LNA) refer to Pay's later opposition to the government. See Pres. Arthur Barclay to P.G. Lamardine, Commissioner Zorzor District, March 7, 1911; Barclay to Rev. W.M. Beck, Muhlenberg Mission, March 10, 1911; Barclay to Commissioner Z.R. Kennedy, Bopora District, March 17, 1911; Barclay to Commissioner P.G. Lamardine, April 1, 1911;Barclay to N.W. William, Kametahun, May 22, 1911; Pres. Daniel Howard to Capt. J.A. Stuard, February 12, 1912; Howard to Paul Lamardine, March 12, 1912; Howard to Lt. J.B.R. McGill, August 4, 1912; all in Executive Mansion Correspondence 1905-1912.

23. See Richard Fulton, "The Kpelle Traditional Political System," pp. 1-19

his jurisdiction. The loi kalong was also the symbolic and ritual leader in religious sacrifices performed for the town as a whole. The one conspicuous difference between Sanoyea and other Kpelle chiefdoms was the absence of the Poro Society.

According to the Kpelle ideal, each chiefdom should have one Poro lodge headed by the local elders. In practice this did not always work out as recently settled and smaller chiefdoms usually lacked lodges.[24] Fulton believes that the lack of a lodge created a "spiritual and thus political dependence," on those chiefdoms with lodges but this does not seem to have been the case in Sanoyea.[25] I can trace no political dependence on the areas with which Sanoyea had strong, usually subordinate, religious ties. Sanoyea was religiously subordinate in that it did not have full control over its religious activities and organizations. For example, there was no local lodge to which Sanoyea parents could send their children for Poro training. The people of Sanoyea had to wait until a school was held in some other district.[26] These religious linkages were not translated into political control nor did the Poro lodges of other places seem to have any influence on local political decisions.

----

24. Richard Fulton, "The Political Structure and Functions of the Poro in Kpelle Society," American Anthropologist 74 (1972): 1224.

25. Richard Fulton, "The Political Structure and Functions of the Poro in Kpelle Society," p. 1224.

26. Interview with Peter Gidding, January 19, 1977.

The lack of a grove did not mean that the local political order lacked religious legitimization. Membership in the Poro was still the norm for full citizenship within the community and almost all Sanoyea Kpelle belonged to the Poro.[27] People expected their political leaders to officiate at corporate sacrifices and the political leaders were the acknowledged spiritual leaders of the community.[28]

Control of the higher Poro offices was reserved for the elders of the community where the lodge was located, but groups like the Sanoyea Kpelle also established a hierarchy of officials for their contingents.[29] Elders and political leaders could, therefore, exercise their control of economic resources through religious institutions and ceremonies.

The important difference in Sanoyea was that the ruler did not have a coercive religious organization to support him in times of crisis or to challenge and check him in times of disagreement. Sanoyea's ruler was more on his own than Kpelle rulers in other areas. In this light Siwi's accomplishments seem even more impressive. Sanoyea had been newly settled and its population was composed of groups from many other places. Siwi had accomplished the difficult task of creating a sense of unity and binding all the groups

----

27. Interview with Amanda Gardiner, March 3, 1977.

28. For a detailed account of one of these rituals see Moses Giddings, "Medicine Boy's New Path, " Foreign Missionary 75, 4 (April, 1955.)

29. Interview with Nee Pee, March 18, 1977.

together. Before Siwi, the area had no established ruling lineage and no historic tradition to unite it. Siwi's creation of a Kpelle state without a local religious organization to support him was a remarkable achievement.

While Siwi built his state in the latter part of the 19th century, the small Liberian state on the coast was growing and becoming more interested in the hinterland. The first Afro-American immigrants set foot on what was to be Liberian soil on April 25, 1822. These first immigrants were free Afro-Americans rather than freed slaves and many of them were professional people with little agricultural experience. Faced with the poor soils, unfamiliar climate and tropical diseases, the colonists were hard pressed to survive.[30] Africans had adapted their agriculture to the crops which grew best in the environment: plantain, bananas, yams, rice, corn, cotton, cassava, beans, vegetables and fruits. The settlers did not adopt the African slash and burn methods of farming and found the techniques they were most familiar with -plows and harrows- almost useless in the rocky soil.[31]

Although they were of African descent, the Afro-Americans had been acculturated and reflected the values of the American culture with which they were

----

30. Tom W. Shick, Behold the Promised Land, (Baltimore: The Johns Hopkins University Press, 1977, 1980), pp. 26-27.

31. Monday B. Akpan, "The Liberian Economy in the 19th century; The State of Agriculture and Commerce," Liberian Studies Journal 6, 1 (1975): 6.

most familiar. For example, they preferred American foods to the crops which could be grown in Liberia.[32] Moreover, they reflected the racism and slavery which they had undergone in America. Even after freed slaves started to make up the majority of immigrants they did not want to farm because it reminded them of their former slave status.[33] Most of the early colonists, therefore, turned not to agriculture but to trade to earn their living. They began to trade American and European products to Africans who lived near the settlements. They bartered tobacco, gunpowder, firearms, salt, cotton cloth, iron pots, beads and rum to the Africans for forest products like palm oil, rice, camwood, ivory, hides and gold.[34] They sold the African products to passing ships or shipped them back to the United States. The first contact between the settlers and the hinterland peoples was, therefore, through trade.

The Afro-American settlers adopted thoroughly American attitudes towards the Africans and their culture. They saw themselves as bearers of "Christianity and civilization" in benighted Africa.[35] To distinguish themselves from the Africans they adopted an "exaggerated often pompous"

----

32. Monday Akpan, "The Liberian Economy," p. 4.
33. Monday Akpan, "The Liberian Economy," p. 4.
34. Monday Akpan, "The Liberian Economy," p. 4.
35. Tom Shick, Behold the Promised Land, passim.

lifestyle.[36] They expected Africans to learn from them, to emulate them and to renounce their traditional ways.

Despite the settler disdain for African culture the Americo Liberian society was organized around institutions analogous to those in African societies. Kinship relations formed the basis for Americo Liberian settler life and economics. The Americo Liberians combined the American family stucture of tracing descent through both father and mother with the African extended family system.[37] Capital moved through this kinship network much the way labor obligations bound Kpelle kinship groups together. The wealthiest member of the family usually became the family head. He would redistribute wealth to help other family members in their careers. Members of a family would help each other in business as well. In times of crisis or death a family member would ensure that a business stayed within the family and that indigent members of the family were taken care of. Wills show that the family head usually tried to see that wealth was equitably redistributed upon his death.[38]

Families were augmented by adoption and a system of wardship, in which a wealthy patron would take on the care of a client's child. Illegitimate children

----

36. Tom Shick, Behold the Promised Land, p. 53.

37. J. Gus. Liebenow, Liberia: the Evolution of Privilege, (Ithaca, N.Y.: Cornell University Press, 1969), p.16.

38. Tom Shick, Behold the Promised Land, pp. 45-53.

-"outside children" as they are known in Liberia- were often acknowledged and brought into the household.[39] The wealthy Americo Liberians also used marriage ties to consolidate wealth, status and political influence.[40]

The Americo Liberians had their counterpart to the Poro Society. The first Masonic Lodge was founded in 1851 and the upper levels of the Liberian elite soon controlled the upper echelons of the fraternal order. The secrecy surrounding the inner circle of the Masons enhanced the status of the Liberian elite much as the secrecy of the Poro did for the Kpelle elite. The Americo Liberian elite used the Masonic lodge as a place to iron out disputes in private just as the Kpelle elders used the Poro bush.[41]

Although the concepts and institutions of religion differed among the Americo Liberians and the Kpelle, religion played an important role within each society. The American Colonization Society had seen the colonization project partly as a method to spread Christianity to Africa. This emphasis on evangelization led to a link between religious position and political authority in Liberia from the very outset. Samuel Bacon, the United Sates agent who went to Sierra Leone to help negotiate the puchase of land for the colony, was an Episcopal minister. Bacon

----

39. Tom Shick, Behold the Promised Land, pp. 99-100.
40. Tom Shick, Behold the Promised Land, p. 50.
41. Tom Shick, Behold the Promised Land, p. 57.

thought that the new colony would "wear rather the aspect of a missionary institution."[42] From 1822-1847 the American Colonization Society sent white agents to govern the black colonists. There were many clergymen among the white agents sent by the American Colonization Society to govern the colony in its early years. For example, Jehudi Ashmun, the white agent who guided the colony through the first difficult years from 1822-1828, was a Congregational minister as well as a journalist.[43]

Several of the black community leaders were also ministers. In the United States black separatist churches offered some of the few opportunities for Negroes to rise to leadership positions. Bright young blacks with leadership potential often entered the clergy and provided leadership in their American black communities. These same men filled the responsible leadership positions within the colonial community. Lott Carey, a black Virginian minister, had been ordained while still a slave. He replaced Ashmun as the leader of the colony after Ashmun's health failed.[44] These black clergymen helped lead the opposition to white rule. They continued to hold leadership positions when the colony gained its

----

42. Samuel Bacon to Col. McCarthy, Governor of Sierra Leone, March 12, 1820 in Charles Huberich, The Political and Legislative History of Liberia, 2 vols. (New York: Central Book Company, 1947) 1:87.

43. Charles Huberich, Political and Legislative History of Liberia 1:292-293.

44. Charles Huberich, Political and Legislative History of Liberia 1:367.

independence from the American Colonization Society.

Most of the early colonists were either Baptists or Methodists because of the work which these churches had done among blacks in the United States. On the first ship bringing colonists to Liberia, the colonists formed the first churches- a Baptist one and a Methodist one. The first missionary group, the Protestant Episcopal Mission Society, was also formed on that first ship. In 1827 the Providence Baptist Church became the first church built on Liberian soil. John B. Pinney, a white resident agent, brought a fourth denomination when he arrived in 1833. He became the first Presbyterian missionary to Liberia and helped start a new church.[45]

These churches provided a focal point for activities outside the household, but more than this they helped instill in the elite a sense of a responsibility for "social uplift." The churches organized benevolent societies to care for the poor and indigent colonists. The churches encouraged a paternalistic attitude toward Africans by reminding the colonists that they had a duty to spread "Christianity and civilization" to Africa.[46]

The colonists combined their social responsiblity with their own self interest particularly in their dealings with the Africans who worked for them. They

----

45. Charles Huberich, Political and Legislative History of Liberia 1:478.

46. Tom Shick, Behold the Promised Land, p. 53.

pursued a policy of assimilation in which they would adopt or buy African youths to acquaint them with Americo Liberian "habits, manners of conduct, [and] religion."[47] The settlers obtained children from the war captives and refugees who drifted into the settlements from the internecine wars of the interior. Sexual liaisons between Americo Liberians and Africans produced illegitimate children who sometimes joined the Americo Liberian communities.[48] African parents saw the Americo Liberians as powerful patrons who offered their children the possiblity of an education and advancement.

Some settlers did see that their charges received an education, but too many others used the assimilation policy as a method of securing cheap domestic labor. Few of these children ever received any formal training in agriculture or animal husbandry even though the Liberian constitution had declared that the government should promote "the improvement of agriculture and animal husbandry among the native population."[49] Even the president of Liberia had to admit that African education, "in many cases was neglected because its importance to the future nation was not perceived and indeed the native was not taken seriously as a factor

----

47. Arthur Barclay, Inaugural Address, (Monrovia: Government Printer, 1904), p.11.

48. Tom Shick, Behold the Promised Land, p. 100.

49. Charles Huberich, Political and Legislative History of Liberia 2:1228.

in the making of said nation."[50]

As the colony grew, colonists opened up new settlements along the St. Paul river. These up river settlements brought them into contact with different African groups like the Gola. It also opened up slightly better land for cultivation. During the latter half of the nineteenth century, the settlers found that they could grow coffee for export profitably if they could attract enough labor. Recaptured Africans, those who had been taken off slave ships by the American Navy before they had reached the New World, provided one source of labor. Some Kpelle and members of other inland groups also moved down into the Americo Liberian settlements to get jobs during their "off" season- between one harvest and the preparations at the beginning of the next growing season.[51] Others lived permanently in the settlements working as farm hands or domestic servants.

The up river settlements had more frequent and prolonged contacts with the indigenous people than the Monrovia settlements. As a result they adapted better to the African environment. They had more social and economic ties with their African neighbors. Although formal treaties defined their political relationships with African leaders, these were augmented by the traditional African methods of creating social and kinship ties as well. African leaders gave wives to the settlers and children for them to raise as their

----

50. Arthur Barclay, <u>Inaugural Address</u>, p. 11.
51. Monday Akpan, "The Liberian Economy," p. 23.

wards.[52] These links enmeshed the settlers in a network of social obligations.[53]

The settlers became dependent on the lucrative trade along the Mandinka-Gola trade route through Bopolu and local trade connections with their neighbors. The up river settlers had adjusted to a Liberian diet and subsisted on rice purchased from their neighbors. The coffee plantations- the basis of the up river economy- depended on a steady supply of African labor.[54]

The increased interaction between Africans and Americo Liberians also caused more friction between the groups. The up river settlements were particularly vulnerable to instability. Disputes between Americo Liberians and the African population and within the African communities could cut off trade and disrupt the labor supply. Although such disputes had occurred since the founding of Liberia, the situation appeared particularly acute to the settlers between 1880 and the end of the century. During these decades the St. Paul river settlers lost ground to foreign competition on two economic fronts. European traders, particularly Germans, were replacing the Americo Liberians as the principal traders in the interior.[55] At the same time

----

52. Tom Shick, Behold the Promised Land, p. 99.

53. Warren D'Azevedo, "Tribal Reaction to Nationalism (part 1)" p. 19.

54. Tom Shick, Behold the Promised Land, p. 98.

55. Monday Akpan, "The Liberian Economy," p.13.

world coffee prices slowly declined and Brazilian coffee came to dominate the world market.[56]

Events in the interior had reached a crisis point during these decades. Conflicts between the Gola and Mandinka became more acute and common. The last strong leader of the Mandinka-Gola coalition at Bopolu died in 1871. His death created uncertainty and set off a new wave of competition among the small chiefdoms for control of the southern end of the trade route.[57]

In the early 1890's marauding horsemen, who were formerly part of Samori of Guinea's army, entered the area. Tensions rose as each Gola chief accused the other of collaborating with these invaders to attack the other chiefdoms.[58]

The settlers themselves also became involved in these disputes by trying to adjudicate disputes among African chiefdoms. In one instance the local magistrate heard a complaint which one Gola man brought against another for stealing his wife and refusing to return her. The magistrate sent three men to arrest the culprit, but the local chief prevented the arrest and detained the three settlers. The Liberian President became involved in this incident and while his agent negotiated for the release of the men, rumors of Gola attacks on the settlements spread through the

----

56. Tom Shick, Behold the Promised Land, p. 116.
57. Tom Shick, Behold the Promised Land, p. 93.
58. Warren D'Azevedo, "A Tribal Reaction to Nationalism (part 2)," Liberian Studies Journal 2, 1 (1969):43.

area. The president authorized the use of the militia; the Gola chief was eventually arrested and the men freed.[59]

Such incidents and the tensions in the area caused the up river settlers to press the government in Monrovia to bring the Africans under some kind of control or to give them arms to do so. The Monrovian settlers had always been ambivalent about trying to establish control over the hinterland and reluctant to commit funds to the project. The government had been discussing extending their control into the hinterland ever since the colony had become a republic in 1847.[60] The legislature had even created an Interior Department in 1869, but more pressing concerns prevented the act's implementation for twenty years.[61] With limited resources the Liberian government paid attention only to areas of immediate strategic importance. By 1897 the situation in the areas adjacent to the Americo Liberian settlements and along the Gola-Muslim trade route through Bopolu, appeared critical. President Cheeseman authorized the use of troops against the Gola and eventually subdued

----

59. Tom Shick, Behold the Promised Land, pp. 93-98.

60. See Monday Akpan, "The African Policy of the Liberian Settlers, 1841-1932 A Study of the Native Policy of a Non-Colonial Power, " Ph D. dissertation, University of Ibadan, 1972 and "Black Imperialism: Americo-Liberian Rule over the African Peoples of Liberia, 1841-1964, " Canadian Journal of African Studies 7, 2 (1973):217-236.

61. Charles Huberich, Political and Legislative History of Liberia, 2:1233.

them.

Two things are significant about this first "pacification" campaign in central Liberia. The government victory was made possible because the southern Gola chiefdoms allied with the government against the northern chiefdoms. The antagonisms among the Gola chiefdoms greatly contributed to the government victory. The southern chiefs submitted to the government in order to gain government patronage and support against other chiefs.[62] African aid would continue to be an essential part of the government's military campaigns. Also, in contrast to the up river settlers, the people of Monrovia were not convinced of the necessity for such interior campaigns. The legislature promptly impeached President Cheeseman and removed him from office.

By 1904 the Liberian government was under pressure from France and Britain to organize its interior policy. The two European powers controlled the colonies adjacent to Liberia and coveted much of the land Liberia claimed. Liberia's finances were in a shambles and the nation was heavily in debt to foreigners. Irate British creditors urged their government to take over the republic if Liberia kept failing to pay its debts.[63] The large powers

----

62. Warren D'Azevedo, "Tribal Reaction to Nationalism (part 2)," p. 47.

63. For a complete history of Liberia's financial difficulties during this period, see George W. Brown, The Economic History of Liberia, (Washington, D.C.: Associated Publishers, 1941.)

challenged Liberian claims on the grounds that Liberia could not effectively control its African population. France and Britain used border attacks as excuses to occupy Liberian territory. By the turn of the century Liberia had helplessly watched France and Britain occupy three quarters of the land Liberia had claimed in 1866.[64] Liberia needed a stronger interior policy both to strengthen its remaining land claims and to derive an income from the African population.

Arthur Barclay became president in 1904 and recognized that he had to make changes to salvage Liberia's future. Barclay appealed for closer ties between the Americo Liberian settlers and the African population. He argued that there were many similarities between the customs of the two groups and that they should be united in one nation.[65] He proposed a new interior administration based upon Frederick Lugard's system of indirect rule in Nigeria. The system created five districts headed by District Commissioners. Important local rulers were to remain in power but also to serve as the government's representatives.[66] Barclay created a Liberian Frontier Force similar to Lugard's West African Frontier Force to replace the ineffective militia which had unsuccessfully tried to stop hinterland wars and maintain communication lines between Monrovia and the

----

64. Charles M. Wilson, Liberia: Black Africa in Microcosm, (New York: Harper Row, 1971), p. 105.

65. Arthur Barclay, Inaugural Address, pp. 10-11.

66. Summarized in Arthur Barclay, Annual Message, (Monrovia: Government Printer, 1909.)

borders. This force was to be trained by Europeans, officered by Americo Liberians and manned by Africans.[67] By 1910 the Frontier Force had 650 men- small by modern standards but comparable to forces in other African colonies.[68] With a military and an administrative system the "pacification" of central Liberia could begin in earnest. The Kpelle were to be one of the first targets.

Benjamin Anderson, the explorer who had visited Sanoyea, foresaw the importance of the Kpelle for Liberia as early as 1874:

> [Kpelle] country is a district populous and fertile enough, but so distracted not by real war, but by petty feuds, that for want of order and quietude it benefits us very little. It is, however, beyond all doubt, the granary of this portion of Liberia and the place from which is to be derived all our manual labor.[69]

Anderson saw the Kpelle as the answer to the two problems that had always plagued the colony: shortages of food and labor. He foresaw establishing the same trade and labor relations with the Kpelle which the up

----

67. Arthur Barclay, Annual Message, (Monrovia: Government Printer, 1907), pp. 12-13.

68. Arthur Barclay to General Padmore, July 8, 1910, Executive Mansion Correspondence 1905 to 1912, LNA, p. 99.

69. Benjamin K. Anderson, Expedition to Musahdu - 1874, p. 40.

river settlements had established with groups like the Gola. Their central location and large population made the Kpelle vital to settler interests. President Arthur Barclay had recognized the importance of the Kpelle in his inaugural address and proposed that Kpelle become the second language of Liberia.[70] Nothing ever came of this proposal and the government's border problems, its financial difficulties, and unrest among the African groups nearest the Americo Liberian settlements prevented the government from turning its attention to the Kpelle. By 1911 the government had signed a border agreement with France, temporarily stabilized its financial position with a foreign loan, and established better relations with nearby African groups. The government, henceforth, could turn its attention to the Kpelle.

By then the southwesternmost Kpelle chiefdoms- Todi, Kakata, Dubli, and Zulu Hills - had developed close relations with nearby St. Paul river Americo Liberian settlements. These Kpelle chiefdoms had developed the kind of ties with the settlers that Anderson had envisioned in 1874. They supplied labor and rice to the settlements and had developed social ties through wardship, adoption, sexual liaisons and marriage. When the government's hinterland administrative system was created, district commissioners were sent to these southern Kpelle and to the Kpelle near the Franco Liberian border. These officials soon stirred up unrest and rebellion with their high handed tactics. As the president admonished

----

70. Arthur Barclay, <u>Inaugural Address</u>, pp. 9-10.

one commissioner:

> I sent you up in the country to help [the chief] mind the country and not to rule the country independently of him...He is the chief of his country and must be so treated. At the trial of all cases in which he is not a party, he must sit with you and you two decide. I can't rule the country by ignoring the chiefs. Most of the trouble of the past has been because some of the commissioners have treated the chiefs in their own country and before their own men as if they were slaves and this had made trouble for the Government, and I will not stand for this in my time.[71]

The policy makers in Monrovia had little control over their subordinates in the field because of the poor communications system. Once in the interior, commissioners and soldiers acted with impunity.[72] The nation's financial difficulties rendered pay unpredictable so that interior service employees took to exploiting the land and the people:

> A settlement between the Liberian Government and the interior native tribes seems no

----

71. President Daniel Howard to Saunders, Sub Commissioner, Zulu Hills, November 18, 1912, Executive Mansion Correspondence 1910-1912, LNA, p. 374.

72. The Executive Mansion Correspondence 1905-1912, LNA, contains several of the presidents' exasperated letters to their lieutenants trying to get them to follow instructions.

nearer than a year ago. The soldiers are unpaid, and in order to get food, [they are] raiding the native villages, burning the houses, taking cattle, pigs, chickens, cassava, rice and whatever else they can find... The native people, driven from the towns, are living in the bush and suffering greatly from hunger.[73]

By 1912 Kpelle land was rife with government troops, rebellious Kpelle bands and rumors of war. The northern Kpelle chiefdoms were trying to organize resistance to the government but the southern chiefdoms, who had strong ties to the Americo Liberian settlements, were reluctant to fight the government. As one missionary reported:

There is great dissatisfaction among the natives further back, and they are said to form a league of the various tribes in order to rise as a unit against the Liberian government. Any tribe refusing to join they threaten with war.[74]

The Sanoyea chiefdom was located between the southwestern Kpelle chiefdoms which had ties to the settlers, and the north and northeastern Kpelle who were opposing the government. Siwi had developed some trade contacts to sell forest products to Americo

----

73. Reverend F.M. Traub, "African Newsletter," Lutheran Church Work 1, 17 (June 27, 1912,) : 8.

74. J.C. Pederson letter, October 18, 1910, printed in Lutheran Church Work 4, 4 (April, 1911).

Liberian merchants from the coast and to sell slaves to European and Vai traders. Sanoyea was still far enough away from the settlements to avoid being entirely within their orbit. Yet, Siwi thought it to his advantage to maintain peaceful relations with them. Siwi died in around 1911 and his son Giting succeeded him. Giting sought to continue his father's expansion of Sanoyea by attacking the neighboring Wallahun Kpelle chiefdom. The arrival of government troops in 1912 forced Giting to decide whether to resist or to submit to the Liberian government. As Giting's son tells the story, Giting reflected on his father's advice:

> when government troops came in there were two pieces of cloth that were presented, red and white. The red was for war, the white is for peace and negotiation. So father [Giting] said "My Pa [Siwi] told me I should not have war with the civilized [Americo Liberia] people. So, I submit.[75]

The other members of the Sanoyea alliance opposed submission to the government. One reluctantly accepted Giting's decision but the other areas split from the group and allied with the Kpelle groups who chose to resist. Giting's foes in Wallahun also submitted so that both Giting and the Wallahun leader received government commissions.[76]

Giting pledged his loyalty in a message sent to

----

75. Interview with Peter Giddings, January 19, 1977.
76. Interview with Peter Giddings, January 19, 1977.

President Daniel Howard, Arthur Barclay's successor. Howard replied and set out the conditions,

> I shall expect you to keep your district peaceful and quiet so that my messenger can always pass freely and also so that everybody can pass freely without being molested. I have heard how some bad commissioners have acted up in the country and all such I shall remove.... If any time any of my commissioners are ordered to fight and call on you to help them, you will be expected to help. I want peace and will do all I can for peace, but the Government laws must be obeyed.[77]

Peace, free passage on the roads and military aid were all that the government demanded of Giting at first and he considered it a small price to pay.

Soon after submitting to the government, Giting faced a new crisis. In a period of difficult communications, rumor often formed the basis for government action. One of Giting's jealous brothers reported that Giting had attacked a group of soldiers.[78] The government feared that Giting had joined the rebellion led by Siwi's former war chief Yakpalo Pay. The government reacted by ordering Giting's arrest and sending troops to fortify nearby

----

77. Pres. Daniel Howard to Chief Giting, July 25, 1912, Executive Mansion Correspondence 1910-1912, LNA, p. 209

78. Interview with Peter Giddings, June 23, 1977.

cooperative rulers.[79] Troops arrested Giting and took him to Monrovia while his family fled because they feared that the government would try to kill all of Giting's potential heirs.[80]

Giting's imprisonment was the low point of his political career, but it was also the beginning of his rise as a master politician. Giting won his case and returned to Sanoyea in 1913 to regroup his family.[81] In the years that followed his return he managed to solidify his position with the government to such an extent that they preferred to rule exclusively through him. The government persuaded Wallahun and other groups to accept Giting as the major liaison with them.[82] The government eventually withdrew the other chiefs' commissions leaving Giting as the sole government chief in the area. Giting had gained control over an area more than twice the size of Sanyea without having to fight.

Giting did not rely solely upon Liberian government support to maintain his position. During these early years of his reign he cultivated marriage and clientage ties with many important local families to solidify his office. The story of Giting's sub-chief Kpaiya illustrates Giting's political shrewdness. Upon

----

79. Several letters in Executive Mansion Correspondence 1910-1912, LNA, especially pp. 318,321,322.

80. Interview with Peter Giddings, June 23, 1977.

81. Interview with Peter Giddings, June 23, 1977.

82. Interview with Mulbah Dangolu, May 3, 1977.

the death of the leader of Bokomu, one of the original members of Siwi's confederation, Giting took the man's grandson Kpaiya to live with him in Sanoyea.[83] Giting raised the boy and thus transformed a potential threat into a loyal dependent client. When Giting became the Paramount Chief in the area, he appointed Kpaiya as the sub-chief of Bokomu. This created a precedent for Bokomu to be ruled by a district chief who resided at Sanoyea under the paramount chief's watchful eye. Such ties with important families became the real cement that ensured Giting's dominance in Sanoyea politics.

Giting tried to create ties with new groups as well. In 1919 Giting heard that a group of Muslim kola traders had arrived in the area from what is now Guinea and he immediately invited them to settle in Sanoyea. He provided the head trader, Nyama Donso, with a house and a Kpelle wife.[84] The Muslims accepted Giting's offer and sent for their families to come and join them. The Muslim community would grow, prosper, and attract more trade to Sanoyea. Although Islam would not gain many converts, elements of Islam would become a significant part of the Kpelle religious system.

Giting received other visitors who were to have a profound effect upon Sanoyea. In 1916 Lutheran missionaries first visited Sanoyea while scouting for a place to locate a new interior mission station.

----

83. Interview with Benda Gwiningali, April 26, 1977.

84. Interviews with Bangali Donso, May 26, 1977 and Peter Giddings, June 23, 1977.

Giting's town did not impress them at first, but they would return some years later.[85]

The American Lutherans had inadvertently started on their course to Sanoyea almost 100 years earlier. Before the mid 19th century, Lutheran missionary efforts in Africa had been scattered and usually short lived. The first Lutheran missionaries were the Danish Moravian Brethren who went to the Gold Coast in West Africa as Danish companies established trading posts in the 17th century. Moravian Lutherans also went to South Africa in 1737 to minister to the Dutch and German Lutherans among the white settlers. A Norwegian Lutheran mission to the Gold Coast in 1779 was the last Luthern attempt to enter the African field until the mid 19th century.[86]

The Lutherans had come to the United States as early as the 17th century and had become part of the expansion westward. Churches grew up around the various immigrant communities throughout the country. Itinerant Lutheran preachers had established their churches in the various settlements. By the nineteenth century the American Lutheran churches were decentralized and very individualistic.

The foreign mission movement among the Lutherans

----

85. "The Burden of Muhlenberg," Muhlenberg Tidings 1,8 (March, 1916): 1. Muhlenberg Tidings was a Lutheran Mission newsletter published between 1915 and 1922.

86. Julius Bodensieck ed., Encyclopedia of the Lutheran Church 3 vols. (Minneapolis: Augsburg Publishing House, 1965) 1:11-17.

became connected with the centralization of the church. By 1820 several small regional associations of Lutheran churches saw the need for a national organization to perform those tasks which were too large or called for more money than the individual congregations could raise. At the same time they feared a national organization that would dictate church doctrine to them. In 1820 they cautiously created a General Synod, a nation wide coalition of Lutheran churches. The General Synod could only suggest, but not prescribe, liturgies, hymnals and catechisms. It could adjudicate on doctrinal disputes only if appeals were brought to it from the congregations.[87]

    The Synod had control only over projects wich did not threaten the local sovereignty of the churches. Its most important work was to establish a seminary at Gettysburg, Pennsylvania and to help organize domestic and foreign missionary work. The distrust for centralized authority prevented the organization of misionary work until 1837. In that year the General Synod created an independent organization to oversee foreign missionary work. The "Foreign Missionary Society of the Evangelical Lutheran Church in the United States" at first simply sent money for a missionary in India. In 1840 it sent out its first

----

87. Abdel Ross Wentz, A Basic History of Lutheranism in America, (Philadelphia: Muhlenberg Press, 1955) pp. 78-79.

missionary to continue the Indian mission.[88]

Liberia was the Foreign Missionary Society's second foreign venture. In 1860 an American Lutheran missionary named Morris Officer had arrived in Liberia from Sierra Leone where he had unsuccessfully attempted to found a mission. To avoid competing with the churches already established in the Afro American settlements, Officer planned to move into the interior of Liberia with some Christian settlers to build a town and school. The Liberian government granted him 100 acres on the St. Paul river about twenty miles inland from Monrovia. He established Muhlenberg Mission Station there in what was then the furthest hinterland penetration of government control.[89] Muhlenberg served as the center of Liberian mission activities for the next ninety years.

Morris Officer had envisioned Christians adopting African children to teach them Christianity, but he found little interest for his proposal among either the Americo Liberians or the African populace.[90] The majority of the first mission children was drawn from those who had no place in the social system or at best an anomalous one. The Liberian government had provided pupils for the mission's first school by indenturing

----

88. A.R. Wentz, A Basic History of Lutheranism in America, p. 110.

89. Reverend J.A. Clutz, "Sketch of Muhlenberg Mission," Lutheran Quarterly 9,3 (July, 1879):449-463.

90. John W. Cason, "The Growth of the Church in the Liberian Environment," PhD. dissertation, Columbia University, 1962, p. 224

forty children from a group of slaves recaptured on the high seas and landed in Liberia.[91] The mission encouraged indenture because it ensured that the mission had complete control over the child's upbringing. African parents who wanted an education for their children but could not afford to pay, also indentured their children to the mission. Americo Liberians would pay for their own children's education at mission schools and sometimes indenture their domestic slaves and illegitimate children by African women.[92] The mission also took in outcast children, the runaways, orphans and strays, who found their way to the station.

The mission accepted day students as well as the boarding students. In 1879, for example, twenty-five out of sixty-two students were day students who lived with their parents in nearby villages.[93] The parents of these children attended church services and were characterized as, "...half civilized and belonging to the better class of the natives, many of them being chiefs or the sons of chiefs."[94] These people offered the missionaries their friendship and politely attended the church, but they did not become Christians themselves. They believed that the new Christian way

----

91. Clutz, "Sketch of Muhlenberg"

92. Examples of these indenture contracts can be found in the Lutheran Church in Liberia Archive, Monrovia. They are usually simple notes saying that the parent has relinquished the child to the mission.

93. Clutz, "Sketch of Muhlenberg."

94. Clutz, "Sketch of Muhlenberg."

was only for their children who were young enough to change.[95] The mission would alternate between the day school and boarding school methods depending on finances, government policy and community support. When money and support were available, the mission preferred the boarding school approach because it gave them more control over their students' lives.

The mission was more than a school and a church to its people; it represented an entirely different kind of life to some, a home for many, an employer and a patron for others. The missionaries knew that many of those who went back to village life after the mission eventually foresook Christianity and returned to African rituals.[96] The mission sought to reinforce its teachings by surrounding its people with a supportive community and separating the Christian community from the surrounding non-Christian communities. As part of the original land grant, Officer had received 200 acres to build a settlement. The mission used this land to create a Christian village by granting five acre plots to graduates of its schools and to some members of its congregations.

The Christian village method of evangelization was popular during the last part of the 19th century. For example, the French Catholic Holy Ghost Society in eastern Nigeria bought slaves, freed them, and developed "freedom villages" in which they lived and worked. The freed slaves would farm for the mission,

----

95. Cason,"Church in Liberian Environment," p. 282.
96. Clutz, "Sketch of Muhlenberg."

attend mission schools and receive religious instruction. Even after the system had to be discontinued because of its expense, the Holy Ghost fathers continued to believe that Christian villages were the best means of evangelization.[97]

The Lutheran mission's most serious problem in these early years was the mortality of the missionaries. In the first eighteen years, fifteen misionaries were sent to Muhlenberg Station. An anguished missionary wrote, "Of this number 3 have died at the mission and one on the way home, 9 have returned with their health more or less shattered, and only 2 remain."[98] Medical care for the missionaries would improve, but the problem of mortality and the constant turnover of missionaries was to leave the brunt of the evangelistic work on the growing numbers of African Christians who worked for the mission.

The Muhlenberg school and church grew from 62 pupils and 55 church members in 1879 to 126 pupils and 197 church members in 1897.[99] By 1900 the mission had started to expand with substations and schools in nearby towns. Muhlenberg, which had been on the leading edge of Americo Liberian settlement, was soon surrounded by new settlements as the frontier kept

----

97. For more details see P.B. Clarke, "The Methods and Ideology of the Holy Ghost Fathers in Eastern Nigeria, 1885-1905," Journal of Religion in Africa 6 (1975):81-108.

98. Clutz, "Sketch of Muhlenberg."

99. Cason, "Church in the Liberian Environment," p. 284.

moving into the hinterland. The Lutherans had wanted to work among the African population rather than among the Americo Liberians, so they decided to keep moving into the interior as the Liberian government extended its control over hinterland peoples. The mission developed an ambitious plan to establish a chain of stations that would eventually stretch to the Franco-Liberian border in Guinea.[100] The first station in this chain, Kpolopelle Station, was built in 1908 on the St. Paul River in the southernmost part of Kpelle country. Further expansion had to wait until the government's "pacification" program had proceeded further.

It is not clear how the missionaries first heard about Sanoyea. A boy from the Sanoyea area, whom the missionaries named Albert Stewart, attended Muhlenberg School. Stewart may have told the missionaries about his home or they may have heard about the town from traders or government officials. A missionary had first visited Sanoyea in 1916 while scouting for a location for a new mission station. He reported that it was a town of about "400 souls."[101] Sanoyea was not their first choice for the new mission station, but after they were refused at other places, they returned to see Giting in 1917.[102] They asked Giting for land

----

100. Reverend. W.M. Beck, "Forward Movement-Muhlenberg," Lutheran Church Work 2,5 (May, 1909):197-200.

101. "The Burden of Muhlenberg," Muhlenberg Tidings 1,8 (March, 1916):1.

102. Interview with Mulbah Gbomokwellie, April 5, 1977.

to build a school and a church to help spread "God's word" to his people. Giting was reluctant to accept the missionaries probably because he was not sure what to make of them. He finally accepted them because he believed that his agreement with the government obligated him to accept the mission.[103] The missionaries were not actually associated with the government but Giting and people afterward would continue to group them in the same category. As I shall argue later, this presumed association would become an important factor influencing conversion. In 1917 it led to Giting's grudging land grant to the mission.

The mission saw Sanoyea as an excellent place for a new interior station:

> The motion to open a new station at Sanoyie was taken up again. Sanoyie had long been thought of as a desirable place to locate. The town of Sanoyie has about 130 huts with an estimated population of 500. It is five days walk from Muhlenberg via Kpolo Pelle or Careysburg. It is in the heart of the Kpelle country and is a strategic place for a Mission. It is the natural place to locate for any one who desires to work among the Kpelle. The people asked for a school and promised to help in opening up.[104]

----

103. Interview with Peter Giddings, January 27, 1977.

104. Mission Council Minutes, January 11, 1917. Sanoyea Mission Records.

So, by 1920 all of the protagonists were in place on the Sanoyea stage. The Liberian government had arrived and though they disrupted Kpelle life very little at first, their demands were soon to increase. Giting had used the government to increase his power just as the government had used him to implement its interior policy. With government aid Giting was able to accomplish his goals and fulfill his father's dream in just a few years.

Two new religious elements had also entered the scene. A Muslim community had begun to grow in Sanoyea and to bring new trade and a new religion. The Muslims established their own cultural enclave within Sanoyea and maintained their own religion and customs. The Lutheran mission created an enclave of its own. The missionaries had built their school and church and Giting had rounded up a few children - mostly slaves - to become their first students. People went to their church out of curiosity, but few people had joined.

On the surface it appeared that little had changed, but several important things had already been determined. The government's goals for Sanoyea would remain political and strategic. They made no plans to draw Sanoyea into a closer relationship with the Americo Liberian settlements, nor did they plan to improve Sanoyea through roads or schools. The government's committment to a policy of indirect rule meant that Kpelle religion and culture were to remain free from government interference. The government had gotten what it wanted - the final authority over the selection of chiefs and the determination of policy.

It was willing to allow local elders jurisdiction over cultural affairs in order to preserve peace by minimizing unnecessary disruptions of Kpelle life. The mission had committed itself to the same evangelistic program it had started at Muhlenberg; it would try to convert people through education and medical care as well as evangelism. The mission would perform the social services which the government did not, but it would also seek to directly change Kpelle culture and religion when the official government policy sought to preserve them.

CHAPTER THREE

Religion and Politics in Sanoyea 1921-1958

The outstanding feature in Sanoyea's history from 1921-58 has been the growth of the town's involvement with the Liberian government and Americo Liberian culture. This involvement grew slowly, affected different segments of the population in different ways, and was focused by the government's policy goals. The government wanted to establish political control over Sanoyea and indeed it created new rules for local politics. Some of these new rules would call for religious and cultural change.

Liberia also wanted to derive revenue from the Kpelle while expending little in return. The government, therefore, did not try to change the system of agricultural production either to increase productivity or to promote economic development. The family would continue to be the basic economic group and the Kpelle would still organize their lives around the rice cultivation cycle. The government's demands for labor and taxes fell hard upon the Kpelle, however, because there were no plans for a compensatory increase in agricultural productivity to offset the increased government demands.

The culture of the politically dominant Americo Liberians- their education, language, dress and religion- would have a great appeal for both the people who wanted to enter local politics and those who simply wanted their children to escape the harsh conditions they faced. Access to the limited political and economic opportunities open to the Sanoyea Kpelle came to depend upon association with Americo Liberian culture. The Lutheran mission became the outpost of Western culture in Sanoyea. The missionaries' norms for public behavior became predominant in Sanoyea and the mission became the gatekeeper for entrance into the Americo Liberian culture.

In this chapter I will trace the development of social and political forces which pushed the people of Sanoyea toward accepting the mission and Christianity. To do so, I will at times need to discuss events happening far away from Sanoyea. Liberia's interior policy was to a great extent a reflection of the problems with its foreign policy. I have already discussed how challenges from France and England spurred Liberia's push into the interior. Foreign pressures would also lead to reorganizations of the interior administration which had important repercussions in Sanoyea.

Chief Giting's agreement with the Liberian government brought Sanoyea under government control but by no means ended Kpelle resistance in the area. The larger, more powerful Jokwele Kpelle- who lived west of Sanoyea- refused to accept government hegemony and carried out a prolonged resistance. Sanoyea served as a military base for government forces until the last rebellious Kpelle had been subdued. The town did not return to peacetime footing until after Giting had died in 1921. The exigencies of war delayed the establishment of a working relationship between government officials and Kpelle leaders.

Giting's son Gbili was the first Sanoyea paramount chief to face the new array of government responsibilities. Regulations promulgated in 1921 specified the obligations each chiefdom had to meet. The people had to pay a hut tax and provide labor for government projects, porters for government officials and provisions for the government's district commissioners. The regulations fixed the amounts and conditions for the collection of these obligations in order to prevent abuse. The regulations also specified which cases could be tried in the chiefs' courts and set fines for adultery, the most common case.[1]

Within these regulations local chiefs could maneuver to their advantage. Gbili, for example, tried to develop a "modus vivendi" which fulfilled his obligations while he benefitted from them as well. A chief could distribute obligations unevenly among his subjects to insure his own advantage. A chief would pass over favored villages whenever labor, porters or supplies were demanded. Other villages, especially those of his political opponents, had to supply labor more often.[2]

The hut tax provided the chiefs' primary source of income and Gbili, like other chiefs, took advantage of tax collection. Some chiefs profited from tax

----

1. Department of the Interior, Regulations Governing the Administration of the Interior of the Republic of Liberia, (Monrovia: Government Printer,1921.)

2. "Minutes of the Nyanfoquellie Conference," 1935, Executive Mansion Correspondence-Interior Department, LNA.

collections by collecting more than once or taking up special collections for local projects that were never done. Gbili was temporarily suspended in 1932 for not submitting all of the taxes he had collected as the government tried to clamp down on tax fraud.[3] His political career would eventually end in a dispute over taxes.

Gbili tried to use all of the powers at his disposal to duplicate the power and wealth his forebearers had accumulated. He continued his father Giting's participation in Liberia's internal slave trade. Like his father, he served mostly as a middleman, buying slaves, holding them and then selling them to slave traders or labor recruiters. When tax time grew near or court fines had been levied , people would pawn their relatives to wealthy men like Gbili in order to get cash.[4] The slave trade could, therefore, continue even after the internecine wars had stopped. Gbili not only recruited men for government projects, he also supplied laborers to the Firestone plantation that opened in 1927. Some workers went to Firestone voluntarily, but others went because they believed it was another government obligation. The workers would remain at Firestone for an unspecified period of time while Gbili and the other chiefs received fees for each man they sent. The difference between slave trading

----

3. "Revenue Agent's Report- 1932," Executive Mansion Correspondence- Interior Department, LNA.

4. Interview with Peter Giddings, January 19, 1977.

and labor recruiting became a fine one.[5]

Government officials also tried to use the system to enrich themselves. District commissioners were supposedly appointed to protect the chiefs' rights against infringement by traders or travelers, to assist commerce, to promote agriculture and to insure that no outsider interfered with local sacred institutions. The regulations specifically defined the quantity of labor and supplies the commissioners were to extract from the people. The regulations forbade officials from accepting gifts from chiefs, taking women to government posts unless a dowry had been paid, and engaging in trade for their own benefit.[6] Several commissioners ignored the prohibitions and used public labor for their private farms. They demanded rice and palm oil above the legal amount and did not reimburse people for goods beyond those required by regulations. Individuals pretending to be government messengers would demand goods or porters and enforce their demands with weapons.[7]

There were constant abuses of the system, but even the "legitimate" demands of the government fell

----

5. Report of the International Commission of Inquiry into the Existence of Slavery and Forced Labor in the Republic of Liberia (Washington D.C.: Government Printing Office, 1931), pp. 125-126.

6. Regulations- 1921.

7. Raymond L. Buell, The Native Problem in Africa 2 vols. (New York: MacMillan and Company, 1928) 2:782-784 and interview with Peter Giddings, January 27, 1977.

hard upon the hinterland people. The hut tax had to be paid in cash in an economy where money was scarce. To get cash people had to leave their homes to work on Americo Liberian farms or, after 1927, at the Firestone rubber plantation. Government labor obligations also took men away from their homes, sometimes during the farming season. Although women performed much of the farm work, the men had to prepare the farms by felling trees and burning brush. Labor recruitment, therefore, had a deleterious effect on agricultural production in the villages.

Labor recruitment was not only time consuming, it could become very brutal. People were supposed to provide transportation for government officials by toting them in hammocks along bush trails. As one former porter remembered

> ...the torch that the soldier had...he used the torch on our heads and on our backs. You see all these burn marks on my back or on my head, that's from the time we were doing the laborer business in this area.[8]

A 1929 League of Nations investigation of slavery in Liberia uncovered many similar abuses. In 1914 Liberia had entered into an agreement with Spain to send Liberian laborers to the island of Fernando Po- a Spanish possession off the coast of equatorial Africa. Labor recruiters, Liberian government officials and some chiefs received payment for supplying these laborers. The harsh treatment afforded the laborers in Fernando Po and the involvement of high government

----

8. Interview with Benda Gwiningali, April 26, 1977.

officials soon brought charges that Liberians engaged in an international slave trade. Similar charges were made against the Firestone plantation labor recruitment system and the government's forced labor program. A League of Nations commission absolved the Liberian government of engaging in slave trade, but nevertheless found a host of abuses by government personnel. The commission recommended the cessation of the forced labor program, the removal of all district commissioners, and their replacement by Americans or Europeans.[9]

Charles King, Liberia's president in 1929, did not accept all of the commission's recommendations, but he did terminate the Fernando Po agreement and issued a proclamation banning slavery and human pawning in Liberia. In the uproar that followed the commission's report King resigned leaving the government in the hands of the Secretary of State, Edwin Barclay. Barclay's administration recognized the importance of reforming the interior administration. A circular letter from the Secretary of the Interior to his department stated,

> You are aware, no doubt, of the mean and ugly things that were said by the League of Nations about this country in the administration of its interior affairs. You

----

9. Commission of Inquiry Report, p. 7. For a more detailed examination of the Fernando Po scandal see I.K. Sundiata, Black Scandal, America and the Liberian Labor Crisis, 1929-1936 (Phildelphia: Institute for the Study of Human Issues, 1980).

are also aware, no doubt, of the shameful light in which this report has placed Liberia before the world. Whether our autonomy will thereby be shaken or not it certainly affects our efforts, our prestige as a government, and calls for...very strenuous [efforts] on the part of government officials in particular to take away this shame.[10]

Although Barclay issued a new set of Interior Department regulations in 1931, the problem with the hinterland service had not really been the laws on the books but the lax enforcement of them. Barclay fired many of the old officials and reorganized the service so that all officials were under closer supervision. Officials had to submit quarterly reports on their subordinates and the presidential correspondence shows that Barclay kept a watchful eye on the department.[11] Barclay demanded that officials obey the regulations to the letter and he held periodic conferences in the hinterland to check on them. The new president realized that Liberia's future depended on its handling of the interior and his administration marked a turning point for the people of the hinterland.

The Barclay administration's close supervision of

----

10. Secretary of the Interior to County Superintendants, Provincial Commissioners, District Commissioners, Paramount Chiefs and Clan Chiefs engaged in the Interior Service, February 18, 1932, Interior Department Correspondence, LNA.

11. Executive Mansion Correspondence-Interior Department, 1931, LNA.

the Interior Department allowed local chiefs to exercise checks on their superiors' power. Each chiefdom was headed by a paramount chief who answered to the government's district commissioners. Each paramount chief had several district chiefs called "clan chiefs" serving under him. In Sanoyea first five, and then later six clan chiefs were responsible to Gbili for maintaining order in their districts. Within each district important towns also had their town chiefs. Large towns like Sanoyea would have even another lower level of chief- the ward or quarter chiefs responsible to the town chief. Once the Interior department started keeping a close eye on its minions, town and district chiefs could complain and get a paramount chief fired. Paramount chiefs could also complain and get unscrupulous district commissioners fired. As the government paid more attention to the interior and the chief's complaints, the power of the chiefs increased and local politics began to heat up.[12]

Gbili's political career ended in one such dispute with his district chiefs. In 1938-9 smallpox broke out in the Sanoyea area. Although the district chiefs had already collected the hut tax, the

----

12. The periodic conferences held by the President or the Secretary of the Interior provided a forum in which such disputes were aired. The Liberian National Archives contained extensive minutes from one such conference held in a chiefdom bordering Sanoyea but in which the Sanoyea chiefs did not participate. These minutes serve as an example of how this process worked. "Minutes of Nyanfoquellie Conference-1935", Executive Mansion Correspondence Interior Department.

government refused to accept it until after the smallpox epidemic had passed. Somehow the tax never reached the government. Gbili claimed that he had returned it to the district chiefs while the chiefs claimed that Gbili had kept it for himself. Concerted opposition from the district chiefs and their complaints to the district commissioner forced Gbili to resign. Gbili tried to appoint his brother Peter Giddings to succeed him, but the chiefs demanded an election in which all of the chiefdom's elders would vote. The Giddings' well-oiled political machinery prevailed and Peter won the election.[13]

The power of the local political offices open to the Kpelle was, therefore, increasing after 1930. At the same time the ability to be effective within local government was coming to depend on how much one knew about the Americo Liberians and their world. Literacy became a skill needed by government functionaries. Those chiefs not themselves literate had to rely on literate clerks who came to wield a great deal of political power. The people who possessed the necessary skills and knowledge were the people educated by the mission. The 1930's and 40's therefore also saw the growth of a mission educated political elite.

One important group was left out by this growing dependence of local politics on knowledge of Americo-Liberian culture and literacy. While the Kpelle community in Sanoyea had worked out its political and cultural relationships with the Americo

----

13. Interview with Peter Giddings, January 19, 1977.

Liberians, the Sanoyea Muslim community developed as a politically and culturally separate enclave. Although nominally subject to the local Kpelle rulers, the Muslims had a separate, parallel system of clan and paramount chiefs which the government used to communicate to them. The Muslims and the government clashed over the regulation of commerce. The Edwin Barclay administration tried to prevent bartering and encouraged the Muslims to pay cash for their trade goods. The government believed that the barter system did not develop the economy because the Muslims bartered Liberian goods for goods produced in Guinea without bringing any cash into the Liberian economy. According to the government the Muslims siphoned off Liberian agricultural products without doing any productive work in Liberia. Muslim traders also evaded government licensing fees by avoiding the main roads and check points, swapping licenses among themselves and using out-dated licenses.[14] Thus, relations between the government and the Muslims were not always cordial.

The Muslims, mostly Malinke and Guinean Kpelle, maintained their cultural distinctiveness by living together in one section of town and by assimilating Kpelle into the Muslim's culture rather than vice versa. Whenever a Muslim took a Kpelle wife, the woman converted to Islam and the children of such a union were raised as Muslims. The Muslims and their children did not belong to the Poro or any of the other Kpelle

----

14. "Revenue Agent's Report-1932," Executive Mansion Correspondence, LNA.

secret societies. Rather than sending their children to the mission school, most Muslims preferred to send them to a Koranic teacher who trained them to memorize verses from the Koran and taught them enough Arabic to write a few verses.[15]

Like many successful ethnic minorities, the Sanoyea Muslims encountered jealousy and resentment among their hosts. This resentment boiled over in the 1930's while Chief Gbili attended a government conference. A Kpelle crowd stormed the Muslim community leader's house to loot it of trade goods and the supposed wealth stored there. The Muslims managed to stave off the attack and send a messenger to Gbili. Gbili arrived a day or so later with troops but by then the situation had calmed down. The Sanoyea elders claimed that some itinerant thugs attacked the Muslims, but after talking to an angry Gbili, they contritely gave the Muslims some women as a peace offering.[16] As in most such situations, the Muslims served as a scapegoat for rising tensions. They had prospered in commerce while the Kpelle, who did not particpate in commerce to any great extent, were feeling the tax burden rather heavily. Although no further attacks occurred, a smoldering resentment of the Muslims continued.

Relations between the Muslim community and the Lutheran Mission were also somewhat ambivalent. The Muslims saw themselves as natural allies with the

----

15. Interview with Bangali Donso, May 26, 1977.

16. Interview with Mulaba Keita, June 22, 1977.

mission in some senses. They felt that both groups were worshipping the one true God and recognized many common prophets.[17] They saw, however, that the mission represented and inculcated cultural values different from their own and they feared that their own culture would be lost if their children attended school and absorbed the Christian teachings. The Muslims, therefore, at times attended the Christian services and at times drew back from the Christians and would not allow them to proselytize in the Muslim quarter. They also preferred to send their children to the Koranic schools rather than the mission schools so that few Muslim children became literate in English.[18] Muslim traders continued to control Sanoyea commerce and to participate in agriculture to some extent, but the Muslim community did not participate in the new political and economic opportunities that were opening up for the Kpelle. The Muslims would remain aloof from much of the interaction among the mission, the Sanoyea Kpelle and the Liberian government.

The late 1930's saw the rise of a new Kpelle political elite which was formed in two ways: through the arrival of educated outsiders and the growth of a local educated group. John Barclay, of Kilibe town within Sanoyea chiefdom, is an example of the first process. A group of immigrants from the Gbalein Kpelle chiefdom north of Sanoyea, had come to the Sanoyea area sometime between 1906 and 1912. They had settled in a

----

17. Interview with Amanda Gardiner, June 10, 1977.
18. Interview with Bangali Donso, May 26, 1977.

spot given them by the local chief who was a distant kinsman. When the Liberian government took over and started to demand taxes and labor, many people wanted to leave the area and return to their original home. The leaders decided that if they stayed they would need a man experienced in dealing with the Americo Liberians. They sent to the Americo Liberian settlements near the coast for John Barclay, a kinsman who had received a grade school education at a Methodist mission there.[19]

Barclay received a triumphant welcome when he arrived and promptly became the area's subchief- an office that later became district chief. His administration proved particularly harsh and he was soon dismissed. After his dismissal, however, he remained an important member of the town and soon convinced it to withdraw from the district which had just dismissed him and annex themselves to a neighboring one. The bitterness of his dismissal and the severity of his administration had ended his political career in that district. Although he did not seek office again, his family became an important political group within the new district. Barclay's son and grandson eventually became district chiefs there.[20] John Barclay's literacy skills and familiarity with the Americo Liberians enabled him to enter the local political game and to establish a new ruling clique within Sanoyea chiefdom.

----

19. Interview with James B. Cooper, April 13, 1977.
20. Interview with Benjamin Barclay, April 5, 1977.

The career of Peter Giddings' demonstrates how a local educated elite can arise. Peter was an important member of Sanoyea's ruling family. His father, Giting, had intended to make Peter his successor, but Peter chose to go to the mission school against his father's wishes. When Giting died in 1921 it was Gbili rather than Peter who succeeded Giting. He finished fourth grade at Sanoyea in 1922 and went to Muhlenberg Station to continue his education. In 1928 Peter returned to Sanoyea after teaching in a mission school for a while. Gbili needed Peter's literacy skills so Peter became the chiefdom clerk. In 1932 Kpaiya, the Sanoyea district chief and the last link to the Sanoyea of Giting's time, finally died in office. At Gbili's urging Peter stood for election and became the new district chief. He attended conferences with Gbili, represented Sanoyea in government disputes, surveyed the kingdom's boundaries and performed all the tasks requiring reading and writing.[21] He quit to return to teaching after a few years so that Peter was not involved when the district chiefs forced Gbili's resignation in 1939.

Peter Giddings' succession to the paramount chieftaincy marked an important event in Sanoyea political history. In many other Kpelle areas the ruling families avoided sending their children to the mission schools when they first opened. The rulers instead forced others, especially slaves, to send their children to the schools. The first groups of literate people in these areas would come from outside the

----

21. Interview with Peter Giddings, January 19, 1977.

ruling group so that power struggles would develop as literacy skills became prerequisites for government service. In Sanoyea the transition from the old ruling clique to the new educated elite worked smoothly and quickly because Peter Giddings bridged that gap between the two groups.

Peter's administration, 1940-56, was the culmination of the educated elite's rise to power in Sanoyea. Giddings started to appoint people with some education to the clan chieftaincies as they became vacant. He paid more attention to their literacy skills than to their social backgrounds and local political positions. He ignored one man's background as a former slave and appointed him to office because of his character and literacy skills.[22] He tried to build a loyal coterie of people who had the skills he needed to bolster his administration as his father Giting had done before him.

Some of his appointments met with strong opposition from the clan elders. When one clan elected a popular non-literate candidate as its clan chief, Giddings kept pressuring the man, finding him guilty of small transgressions until the man was forced to resign. Against the wishes of the clan elders, Giddings then appointed a man with some education to serve as acting clan chief. Local opposition soon forced the acting clan chief to resign as well and the elders elected another man with no literacy skills.[23]

----

22. Interview with Peter Giddings, January 19, 1977.
23. Interview with Mulbah Wuto, April 13, 1977.

This dispute was not about literate or non-literate chiefs, but rather about who should have the right to choose an area's clan chief. Yet this dispute shows the lengths to which Giddings would go to get members of the educated elite into office. In time, as more people from the clan went to school, they would find their own literate candidates for office.

The 1940's saw Sanoyea also stengthening its ties to the Americo Liberian world in areas other than politics. By the end of the 1930's people started to recognize that limited economic opportunities were opening up for the Kpelle within the Americo Liberian world and that their participation in them depended upon going to school.[24] The Lutheran Mission provided a few jobs as teachers and evangelists for its school graduates. In the middle 1930's the Firestone Plantation, three days walk from Sanoyea, recovered from the world depression in rubber prices and became a viable source of jobs. Although only a few Sanoyea people found good jobs at Firestone, those few were enough to demonstrate what was possible with an education. Most Sanoyea people at Firestone worked as laborers, but one man from the Sanoyea Mission School's first graduating class found work in one of the laboratories at Firestone until Peter Giddings lured him away to become a clan chief in Sanoyea. He became not only an example of the employment opportunities opened up by education, but also demonstrated social mobility. He had once been a slave but used his education to gain political power and later employed

----

24. Interview with Peter Giddings, January 19, 1977.

the skills acquired at Firestone to establish a large, profitable rubber farm.[25] Although there were few such prominent successes, the potential for success would convince many Sanoyea Kpelle to send their children to the mission school.

The 1940's saw Sanoyea building new transportation links with the Americo Liberian world. The Liberian government constructed the first unpaved jeep road joining Sanoyea to the main interior road through Kpelle country. This twenty mile road was only passable during the dry season and would have to be improved many times before it could carry any sizable amount of traffic, but it marked a beginning.[26] The Lutheran mission built an airstrip on the outskirts of town in 1947 so that air travel linked the missionaries to the coast and the other interior mission stations.[27]

By the 1940's and 50's Sanoyea had, therefore, drawn itself more closely into the Americo Liberian world. Ironically, the social changes that the Gidding family had helped introduce into Sanoyea worked to end their political control over the town. The continued recruitment of younger educated people into politics had brought an ambitious new element into the political game. Their presence greatly intensified competition for local offices because there were few outlets for

----

25. Interview name withheld.

26. <u>Foreign Missionary</u> 75,12 (December, 1955):16.

27. Annual Report, Twenty fourth Annual Conference (1948), LCLA.

their ambition. Death, retirement or charges of malfeasance were the only ways to remove local politicians from office. Peter Giddings' political career ended in 1956 when malfeasance charges were brought against him just as they had been brought against his brother Gbili in 1939. Peter tried to keep the chieftaincy within the family by appointing one of his brothers just as Gbili had. The younger element, those educated people outside of the landowning and big man lineages, continued to challenge Giddings' dominance and succeeded in wresting control away when another malfeasance case was brought against the new chief in 1958.[28] A former Giddings protege who had led the assault on Giddings' power became the first paramount chief to come from outside the Giddings family. The Giddings family would remain an important force in Sanoyea politics, but they were no longer dominant. A new era had begun in Sanoyea politics.

The period of Giddings' control had seen the arrival of the Americo Liberians and their culture. Throughout the period Sanoyea became increasingly drawn into a network of ties with the Americo Liberian world. The material benefits of that world became increasingly evident at the same time that the colonial relationship between the Americo Liberians and the African Liberians set distinct limits on the Sanoyea populace's access to those benefits. The Sanoyea elders for example could participate in local politics and the election of local "Native Authorities", but these offices were subordinate to the government

----

28. Interview with Momo Kaine, June 4, 1977.

appointed district commissioners. No Sanoyea person could even hope to have an impact on the national government at this time. However, to the extent that Sanoyeans did have access to this world, the Lutheran Mission was the bridge between the Kpelle world and the Americo Liberian world. The mission taught the skills needed in the Americo Liberian world and in the local manifestations of that world. The mission also taught about the culture associated with that world by demonstrating the proper forms of behavior, dress, and religion. The political and economic context of Liberian colonialism, therefore, made the mission not only the purveyor of a different culture but the purveyor of the culture associated with the dominant group.

Too often colonized people's acceptance of the culture of the dominant colonizers is seen as a rejection of their own culture and either an identification with the colonizers or an "aping" of their ways.[29] This is too simplistic a view of cultural transformation in a colonial situation. The Sanoyea Kpelle did not reject their culture but rather incorporated facets of Americo Liberian culture into an already heterogeneous or pluralistic culture. At the same time, as a reaction to the rising importance of this foreign culture, Sanoyeans also reaffirmed their Kpelle culture with the arrival of the Poro and other secret societies.

----

29. See Franz Fanon's Black Skins, White Masks, (New York: Grove Press, 1968) for a classic polemic representing this view.

Literacy skills and some knowledge of Americo Liberian culture facilitated dealing with the Liberian government, but they never became the sole qualifications for political office. The Sanoyea leaders had to mediate between the demands of the Liberian government and the demands of their constituents. In Kpelle chiefdoms all chiefs had ritual responsibilities and an obligation to follow Kpelle traditions. The "predicament" of the Sanoyea chiefs was to be able to keep one foot in the Americo Liberian world and the other foot in the Kpelle world. During the same period that Peter Giddings was bringing educated people into the government, he, the Sanoyea elders and the new elite also moved to strengthen their ties with other Kpelle organizations. They asked the Poro and other secret societies in the older Kpelle chiefdoms to establish branches in Sanoyea.[30]

With the establishment of its own Poro grove in 1951, Sanoyea reached its maturity as a Kpelle chiefdom. Just as the chiefs had to balance and integrate Americo Liberian and Kpelle cultures in their own lives, Sanoyea chiefdom also had to achieve a balance in its corporate identity. The upstart Sanoyea chiefdom had become an important chiefdom because of its involvement with the Liberian government. The chiefdom had assisted the government in its conquest of other Kpelle chiefdoms. Some other Kpelle chiefdoms had looked upon Sanoyea as somewhat tainted by its

----

30. Interview with Peter Giddings, January 27, 1977.

Americo Liberian contacts.[31] The people of Sanoyea had always considered themselves fully Kpelle and the arrival of their own Poro grove symbolized and asserted their Kpelle identity. Now the older Kpelle chiefdoms as well as the Liberian government had acknowledged Sanoyea's importance and legitimized its status.

The reasons the Sanoyea elite waited this long to get their own grove remain unclear. Peter Giddings, a key figure in the acquisition, said only, "During my paramount chieftaincy, I consulted the others [about whether] we should establish our own. They agreed. Then we went and paid for our bush."[32] There are two plausible explanations for the late arrival of the Poro grove. Since the establishment of a Sanoyea grove would mean a loss of income to the groves where Sanoyea sent its children, the cost of obtaining a grove was relatively high. Although Sanoyea had grown under government jurisdiction, it had not expanded its economic base. The Sanoyea elite quite simply might not have been able to afford a grove until 1951 when the chiefdom had expanded somewhat. Alternatively, other areas' opposition to Sanoyea because of its collaboration with the Liberian government may also have delayed Sanoyea's acquisition of a grove. Only further research will determine the cause of the delay, but whatever the reason, the lack of a grove does not

----

31. Interview with Peter Giddings, January 27, 1977. I also observed this attitude among Kpelle students at the University of Liberia with whom I talked about Sanoyea.

32. Interview with Peter Giddings, January 27, 1977.

mean that the Poro was not present in Sanoyea. All Kpelle belonged to the Poro and believed that the membership in the Poro defined being a "true Kpelle Man."[33] The Sanoyea elders were still the highest ranking Poro members in the town and could use the Poro to enforce their decisions. The arrival of a grove gave the elders the additional power of controlling the initation rites, that is, the socialization process.

Thus, while the colonial situation created an impetus for people to adopt Americo Liberian culture, there were also forces pushing for the maintenance and even expansion of Kpelle culture. The government's protection of the Poro society in its effort to avoid stirring up unrest during the "pacification" period led to the Poro remaining free of Americo Liberian influence for the most part. The penury of the Liberian government prevented them from introducing social services which may have challenged Kpelle institutions. Almost by default the Lutheran Mission became the only organization specifically aimed at altering Kpelle culture. The mission would be hindered not only by the government but also by the local political context and by the structure of Kpelle culture and religion.

----

33. Interviews with Amanda Gardiner, March 3, 1977 and Sackie Nangbora, March 16, 1977.

CHAPTER FOUR
The Sanoyea Mission

Chapter 1 has examined the structure of Kpelle society and religion; chapters 2 and 3 haved looked at the historical context which led to the Lutheran mission's presence in Sanoyea and created conditions for its acceptance. This chapter will trace the history of the Sanoyea mission to show that the encounter between Lutheran Christianity and Kpelle religion was one between competing explanatory, social and cultural systems. Earlier chapters have shown the multifaceted relationship between Kpelle religious behavior and social relations. Political roles required the performance of ritual, individuals performed rituals as members of social groups, religion provided the ideology reinforcing the social system, and religious organizations embodied Kpelleness- the essence of Kpelle culture. To some extent one can make the same argument about the missionaries. To the Kpelle at least, they embodied Western culture, presented an ethic which reflected a different set of social relations, and created new groups and rituals. For example, the Christian values of humility, piety, charity, and the admonitions against greed, ambition and covetousness conflicted with the Kpelle view of human nature on some points, yet on other points reinforced Kpelle views.

Lutheran efforts to convert the Kpelle to Christianity intensified these differences and conflicts. Conversion was not only an intellectual assent to Christian doctrines and ethics, but also a social and cultural choice. In trying to convert people, the mission created intense personal struggles, split individuals from their social groups and attacked the Poro, the central cultural organization in Kpelle life. The nature of the Lutheran attempts at conversion and the reactions of the Kpelle to the conversion process shaped the way Christianity would affect Kpelle religion and society.

To understand this process other scholars have looked at the missionaries themselves to try to reconstruct their consciousness. To do this requires biographical information which was not available for the Kpelle case. No one has done such research in Liberia although it remains a fertile field for future researchers. I will concentrate on the missionary-villager encounter at the point of contact, that is, I will look at what the missionaries actually did, how they and their agents presented the gospel, and the texts they used. This focus will not only reveal the missionaries' goals, strategies and methods, but also how these all changed as the Kpelle accepted or rejected Christianity on their own terms.

This chapter will therefore examine the history of the Sanoyea mission from its opening until 1954, when the station had become a backwater outside the mainstream of mission activity. The rise and fall of the Sanoyea Station provides a portrait of the hopes, activities and problems the Lutherans faced in their concerted effort to change Kpelle religious beliefs. The Lutherans ultimately did not convert any significant number of Kpelle into churchgoing Christians. Nevertheless, as the next chapter will argue, the Lutheran Mission had an important impact on the Kpelle religion far beyond its meager membership rolls. A close examination of the mission's activities and doctrines will help us to understand that impact.

The American Lutheran churches spent a great deal of time and money in Liberia. The Liberian mission was one of only three foreign missions operated by the General Synod of the Evangelical Lutheran Church in the United States of America and Liberia was the only American Lutheran mission field in Africa until the American Lutherans replaced the German Lutherans in Tanganyika and the Cameroons after World War I.[1] By 1933 it had been in Liberia for 73 years and had spent 1.7 million dollars.[2] Only the Protestant Episcopal and the Methodist churches had spent more, and most of their money was spent on the Americo Liberia community. The Lutherans, on the other hand, had concentrated all of their efforts on the Kpelle and the Loma people of the interior. Most of the money was spent in bringing social services, like education and health care, to the indigenous people at a time when the Liberian government had neither the funds nor the inclination to do so.

It is best to begin by considering what the missionaries meant by "conversion." The documents I examined showed more concern with practical matters

----

1. Julius Bodensieck ed., Encyclopedia of the Lutheran Church 3 vols. (Minneapolis: Augsberg Publishing House, 1965) 1:11-17.
2. "Facts and Observations on Liberia, Africa," Foreign Missionary 53,7 (July, 1933) :13.

than with abstract or theoretical concerns. Nevertheless, it is possible to piece together the missionary strategies by looking at their actions. In his study of the Chewa of Malawi, Ian Linden found two competing ideas of conversion. The Catholic White Fathers considered conversion,

> primarily an intellectual assent to the basic Christian truths. The candidate for baptism was given an examination and the catechism answers to such questions as "who is God?", "Who is Christ?", were expected.[3]

In contrast the Methodist missionaries saw conversion as a "personal assent to Christ," rather than instruction in Christian doctrine.[4]

Neither of these categories fully describes the Lutheran mission in Liberia. The Lutherans did indeed require catechal instruction and at the very least some memorization of Martin Luther's doctrines. They had a relatively short instruction period- six months - when compared, for example, to the Episcopal mission in Liberia which required four years of instruction before baptism.[5]

----

3. Ian Linden, Catholics, Peasants and Chewa Resistance in Nyasaland, (Berkeley: University of California Press, 1974), p. 54.

4. Ian Linden, Catholics, Peasants and Chewa Resistance, p 54.

5. Joseph C. Wold, God's Impatience in Liberia, (Grand Rapids, Michigan: William B. Eerdmans Publishing Company, 1968), p. 92.

The Lutherans, however, required more than intellectual assent as well. They expected their converts to reject Kpelle religion and culture and to reflect Christian teachings in their daily lives. Indeed they were often more concerned with the daily activities of their converts than with their knowledge of Christianity. The boy who grew up to be the first Liberian Lutheran bishop was refused readmittance to school after a vacation because he had undergone Poro initiation. They refused to accept someone who "only had one foot in 'civilization'."[6]

Thus, the Lutherans in effect defined conversion as a total cultural transformation. This definition helps us understand the multifaceted strategy and tactics of the Lutheran Mission. The missionary goal in Sanoyea was, in its simplest terms, to "bring the message of Christ" to the local people. The missionaries believed they offered the people a clear dichotomous choice between "superstition" and the "true religion" with no middle ground. Although they viewed Kpelle religion with disdain, their actions show that they recognized the complex functions religion fulfilled within Kpelle society. Kpelle religion provided an explanatory paradigm or a system of underlying causes for events in the real world and an instrumental system, that is, a system of prescribed actions one could take to achieve certain ends. Moreover, many social relations were drawn in terms of religious duties and obligations. The missionaries

----

6. Interview with Bishop Roland Payne, October 22, 1976.

therefore had to meet the challenge of Kpelle religion on several levels.

The mission tried to discredit Kpelle religion by showing that it was ineffective as an explanatory-instrumental system and by offering Christianity and Western medicine as alternatives. Instead of praying to the ancestors to cure infertility, people would be told to pray to God or Jesus. Instead of relying on charms and amulets to cure disease, people would be sent to the mission dispensary. Mission schools would introduce the new paradigms to the young and mission communities would form the basis for new social ties to reinforce mission teachings. This had been the strategy used at the first Lutheran station in the Americo Liberian settlements and it was to be the model for all Lutheran stations in the interior.[7]

Although the missionaries clearly presented Christianity as an alternative to the Kpelle system, nothing intrinsic to Christianity directly refutes or contradicts the Kpelle explanatory system of spirits, medicines and witchcraft. Christianity's long coexistence with magic in the Middle Ages and modern spiritualism demonstrate that the two are compatible. It was science that brought about the decline of magic in Europe, not Christianity.[8] The paradigms of

----

7. See Chapter 2 above.

8. For a detailed description of medieval religious change see Keith Thomas, <u>Religion and the Decline of Magic</u>, (New York: Charles Scribner's Sons, 1971.) An interesting interdisciplinary debate has grown up

microbes and atomic particles have produced the scientific wonders which replaced the supernatural as a system of instrumentality. Using science to discredit Kpelle religion means, moreover, reliance on a long education process and, in practice, means working primarily with children. Although the missionaries did indeed try this in their schools, they could not use it in their attempts to convert non-literate adults. Adults were told that the dispensary's cures were performed by God with the assistance of the missionary medical staff.[9]

Although Christianity could have been intellectually compatible with Kpelle religion, the mission saw no room for compromise in their battle to replace Kpelle religion as an explanatory system. The missionaries kept insisting that accepting Christianity meant rejecting all other religious beliefs and saw any attempt to mix the Kpelle and Christian religions as a hypocritical stance.

On the other hand the Kpelle only accepted Christianity on their own terms and were quite willing to mix the two. Although the Kpelle recognized that prayer to God was an important weapon, they wanted additional means to deal with the hostile world around them. Not only did Christianity fail to refute the existence of spirits and witchcraft, it failed to

---

around Thomas's definitions of magic and religion. See Hildreth Geertz and Keith Thomas, "An Anthropology of Religion and Magic," Journal of Interdisciplinary History 6 (1975): 71-89.

9. Interview with Nee Kani, July 11, 1977.

establish adequate defenses against the supernatural malevolence of others. Kpelle Christians would, therefore, continue to use certain elements of Kpelle religion.

The conflict between the mission and Kpelle religion also affected social groups. The missionaries recognized that Kpelle religion was embedded in social ties and that attempts at conversion would meet with opposition from groups important to Kpelle social organization. The most important of these organizations was the Poro Society. In education the mission and the Poro were in direct competition. The Poro instructed children in the Kpelle explanatory paradigms and those skills necessary to be a Kpelle. The mission tried to teach that those paradigms were worthless and inculcate Western patterns of behavior into children.

Mission strictures against participation in Kpelle rituals created tensions. Individuals underwent intense conflicts trying to fulfill both their social obligations and their mission obligations.[10] The mission tried to provide an alternative set of social relations for those who became estranged from their social groups. They emphasized the distinctive group identity of Christians within their home villages and created entire Christian communities in and around the mission station. Converts were encouraged to convert their families in order to recreate familial bonds

----

10. Mrs. C.E. Buschman, "Wubu, the Conversion of An African Chief's Mother," Foreign Missionary 57 (1937): 18-20.

within the Christian framework. The belief that only Christians would gain admittance to heaven spurred many to try to bring their close relatives into the Church. As one woman said about her afterlife,

> it would not be good for my mother to be sitting somewhere, my grandmother to be sitting somewhere and for me to be sitting somewhere [else.][11]

The Africans who worked at the mission also demonstrated a camaraderie which attracted people to investigate Christianity.[12] It took a while before the sense of Christian community became evident; it was, therefore, not suprising that many of the mission's earliest converts were those whose social relations were weak to begin with- slaves, orphans and outcasts.

Although these intellectual and social aspects of religion were important to the missionaries, they had defined conversion primarily as a cultural transformation. The missionaries believed that they were spreading culture as well as religion. They saw themselves as purveyors of a different and "higher" culture and tried to demonstrate that culture and their way of life whenever possible. As one mission ruefully admitted, the missionaries too often thought that they were there "to civilize, clothe, and polish our people

----

11. Interview with Nee Pee, March 18, 1977.

12. Interview with Amanda Gardiner, March 11, 1977.

into Liberians."[13] They tried to recreate the "comforts of home" as much as possible. The missionaries were creatures of their own culture. To condemn the missionaries for being ethnocentric or cultural chauvinists misses the point. Given the nature of the period in which they lived and the vast difference between Western and African material culture, they could hardly be otherwise.[14] Their culture had provided them with a world view which convinced them that their way of life was ideally suited to the actual state of affairs, but the Kpelle culture did the same for the Kpelle people.

The descendents of American blacks who had come to Liberia shared some of the same cultural roots as the missionaries. Although the Americo Liberians had, of course, descended from slaves taken from Africa, very little of their African heritage was part of the cultural baggage carried to Liberia. For the most part, the black settlers also saw themselves as models which Africans should emulate, but they had taken few steps to narrow the gap. The missionaries however were willing to try to "uplift" Africans and provide social services which the government could not. Moreover, the missionaries were trying to bring the Kpelle into the culture of the dominant political minority- an essential function which has had important long term effects.

----

13. Jennie R. Oberley to E.E. Gersch, October 9, 1934, Sanoyea Mission Records.

14. Interview with Bishop Roland Payne, October 22, 1976.

The mission, therefore, at first provided the accoutrements of their culture along with their religion. In the early years the mission supplied Western style clothes to their students and workers and food and other gifts to people who came to live at the mission. The mission became a paternalistic source of gifts.

> Sanoyea, like most of our other stations, passed through the Santa Claus stage when the mission was looked upon as not much more than a Christmas Tree. I worked there myself ten years ago and doubtless contributed somewhat to that idea.[15]

The mission expected their gifts to be the first step in cultural conversion but the Kpelle saw the gifts as the first step toward establishing a patron/client relationship with the mission. Eventually the Kpelle came to expect gifts from the mission and the mission would have a hard time overcoming its reputation as "Santa Claus." The mission's purpose however was to help divorce people from their own culture and to hasten their assimilation into the missionary's culture. They hoped that their students would "understand that they are fitting themselves to live a life different from that of their people."[16]

----

15. Jennie Oberley to Erle C. Griner, Zanesville, Ohio. October 9, 1934, SMR.

16. Muhlenberg Tidings 2, 10 (April 1919) Lutheran Church in Liberia Archives, Monrovia.

The Lutheran missionaries were, therefore, pursuing a multi-faceted strategy. They wanted to present the Christian explanatory paradigm, discredit the Kpelle paradigm, provide alternative social groupings, demonstrate the advantages of Western culture and transform individuals into cultural replicas of the missionaries themselves. To pursue these strategies, the mission set up an evangelistic program, a school, and a medical facility at Sanoyea. The mission would have internal arguments over which front should be pressed at a given time. The history of the Sanoyea mission illustrates how these strategies and goals interacted.

On February 9, 1917 a committee from the Lutheran mission met with Sanoyea Chief Giting and agreed upon the conditions for the opening of the mission station.[17] The first two years were spent constructing buildings and recruiting boys for the school. The people of Sanoyea welcomed the mission because it provided jobs as laborers and carriers. The mission, however, found it more difficult to recruit children for its school. The mission had decided to use a modified boarding school system in Sanoyea. The students would live at the mission, but their families were required to supply enough food to feed them throughout the school term.

Chief Giting had the responsibility to recruit the first students and he responded by sending several

----

17. *Muhlenberg Tidings* 2, 10 (April, 1919) LCLA, Monrovia.

of his slaves. Neither the chief nor the free commoners wanted to give their children to the mission while it was still an unknown group. Many people feared that Chief Giting was simply selling children to the missionaries as a new form of slavery. They saw children doing chores as part of their school activities and believed that the children were being made the domestic slaves for the missionaries.[18] Such sale of children had been a standard practice and, for some people, the only relationship they had seen between up country people and people from the Americo Liberian settlements. This view of the mission was prevalent even after Chief Giting's own son Peter became one of the first mission students.

The boarding school system soon ran into difficulties. The mission had at first paid for and supplied everything the students needed except food. By 1922 they were having difficulty getting people to supply even food and briefly had to replace the boarding school with a day school.[19] The mission did graduate its first group of five fourth grade students who then continued their education down at the mission's main station.[20] Nineteen twenty-three saw the school attendance reach 53 and a new girl's school

----

18. Interview with Peter Giddings, January 19, 1977.

19. "Report of the 11th African Conference," (January, 1923) p. 21, LCLA.

20. "Report of the 11th African Conference," (January, 1923) p. 21, LCLA

developed.[21] The boarding school approach, however, proved too expensive. So the missionaries tried to stop supplying clothes and school supplies and make the students earn their way.

> We have tried to have the Workers discourage the idea of clothing being so essential and have told them they may have the larger ones wear something of an approach to civilized clothes with the provision that they earn them by doing special work about the place before and after school.[22]

Finally the mission decided to pay for books and the teachers' salaries only and to depend on the children's relatives to provide the rest. As the cost to parents went up, enrollment went down until there was no school at all.[23]

With no one to teach, the missionaries and their African assistants concentrated on the evangelical work. The mission's evangelical program had been a failure from the start. A 1922 report lamented, "the religious work is practically nothing at the station except for the religious instruction given the boys [students]. The people have practically refused to

----

21. "Report of Albert Stewart, Sanoghie Station," (December 26, 1923) LCLA.

22. "Report of the 10th African Conference," (July 1922) p. 14, LCLA.

23. "Sanoyea Congregation Report," (1930) p.3, LCLA.

come to services in the town."[24] The situation improved somehwat as the evangelists continued to preach in the small towns outside of Sanoyea town itself. With more people concentrating on spreading the Gospel to new areas, the mission gradually gained more listeners.

The early failure of the evangelical program and the ups and downs of the educational program contrasted sharply with the quick success of the medical program. The Sanoyea dispensary opened on February 1, 1921 and during the first two weeks treated between 10 and 20 local people and 10 to 15 students and workers each day. A vaccination program proved a huge success drawing entire families including Chief Giting himself.[25] Not only people from Sanoyea town, but people from all the surrounding villages began to flock to the dispensary. The willingness of the Sanoyea Kpelle to accept medical treatment readily suprised the missionaries, although it is not so suprising in retrospect.[26] The Kpelle tended to accept those aspects of alternative religions which fit more closely with their own religious beliefs. The Kpelle "model for reality" allowed the ready acceptance of new medicines whether from Kpelle, Muslim or Christian "medicine men." As time went on the dispensary became an important part of the mission's attraction. Between

----

24. "Report of the 10th African Conference," (July, 1922) LCLA p. 14.
25. Muhlenberg Tidings 3,11 (April,1921): 2-3, LCLA.
26. Muhlenberg Tidings 3,11 (April,1921): 2-3, LCLA

1922 and 1927 the success of the dispensary was the only consistent development at the Sanoyea station.

One of the station's major problems was lack of continuity among the white personnel. During the decade 1920-1930 the Lutheran mission throughout Liberia saw rapid staff turnover. Of the 30 missionaries who served in Liberia, 40 percent served for two years or less.[27] At Sanoyea the problem was particularly acute and at several times the station did not have any white missionaries at all. With this shortage of missionaries, much of the actual work at the station was performed by black workers. These black workers were organized into a hierarchy based upon education. Blacks with at least an eighth grade education were at the top with the title evangelist or teacher. The next rank, composed of less educated people, were called catechists or Christian workers.[28]

Few people from the Sanoyea area had had any previous contact with schools or missions. Consequently, none of the evangelists and only one of the Christian workers at the station came from the Sanoyea area. The lone exception, Albert Stewart, was born in the Sanoyea area but had been raised and educated in one of the Americo Liberian

----

27. Jennie Larmonth Oberley, "Many Changes and Obstacles Explaining Results in Liberia," Foreign Missionary, 48,4 (1928).

28. "Report of Fifth Annual Conference," (1928) p. 3, LCLA.

settlements.[29] Stewart had the most success in arousing local interest in the mission and in 1924-5, for all practical purposes, ran the mission station. His sudden death in 1926 left a void that no one else could fill because no one else had his knowledge of the Sanoyea area and the Sanoyea people. Instead, the evangelists either came from the settlements or, like S.B. Allison, came from Sierra Leone.[30] Except for Stewart, therefore, the religion being preached and the people preaching it were foreigners to the area.

The years between 1917 and 1927 had been lean ones for the mission. The evangelists and Christian workers had gone far and wide but few people attended church regularly. The school had at first expanded but then dwindled as a dispute arose over how much the people expected from the mission and how much the mission felt it should provide. From 1922-27 Sanoyea station had gone from having a school but no church, to having a small church but no school.[31] By 1928 a few hopeful signs began to appear on the horizon. First, Peter Giddings and the other graduates of the mission school's first class began to return to the Sanoyea area. Their return finally convinced people that the schoolchildren had not been sold into slavery.[32] Moreover, because of his education Peter Giddings had been able to work as a school teacher for the mission

----

29. Interview with D.B. Livingstone, June 14, 1977.
30. Interview with Corinne B. Allison, March 8, 1977.
31. "Sanoyea Congregation Report," (1930) p. 1, LCLA.
32. Interview with Peter Giddings, January 19, 1977.

in another town and later got a job with the newly arrived Firestone Rubber Company.[33] People started to realize that the mission school was not only a safe place to send their children, but that once they went to school new job opportunities existed for them. People then started to send their children back to school.

In 1928 Sanoyea also received a permanent white missionary, Rev. David Dagle, who revitalized the foundering station. In 1928-9 a new church was built without using any mission funds. Contributions financed the purchase of building materials, and mission workers, and local people provided the labor.[34] The school began to grow again- from ten students in 1928 to thirty one in 1930. A new government regulation allowed the mission to open day schools in five of the surrounding villages serving a total of 100 students in 1930. Under the day school program each pupil had to pay for his books and supplies while the village paid the teacher's salary and provided a house for the teacher, a schoolroom and a place for prayer.[35] The mission at Muhlenberg- rather than the teachers- set the curriculum for the school. This led to inappropriate texts and some dissension.

...the Reading Course for 1928 was not a

----

33. Interview with Peter Giddings, January 19, 1977.
34. "Sanoyea Congregation Report," (1930) p. 3, LCLA.
35. "Sanoyea Congregation Report," (1930) p. 3, LCLA.

success. Nearly all of the teachers seemed uninterested and those who did even part of the work, did it under pressure. We think most of the [three] books are too difficult, notably "The Life of David Livingstone" and the "Autobiography of Benjamin Franklin."[36]

The curriculum for the First Grade Bible course contained simpler stories whose themes were more familiar to people from a rural environment. These stories told about interfamily squabbles, kings and heroic deeds while emphasizing their religious themes:

1. God Made the World. (Gen.1)

2. Noah and the Ark. (Gen. 6-8)

3. The Stolen Blessing. (Gen. 27)

4. Joseph Sold by His Brothers. (Gen. 37)

5. Joseph Forgives His Brothers. (Gen. 45.)

6. The Birth of Moses. (Ex. 2.)

7. Moses and the Burning Bush. (Ex. 3.)

8. Crossing the Red Sea. (Ex. 14.)

9. The Manna. (Ex. 16.)

10. The Fall Of Jericho. (Joshua 6.)

----

36. "Education Committee Report- Annual Conference, 1928," Sanoyea Mission Records.

11. The Boy Samuel. (1 Sam. 3.)

12. David Anointed King. (1 Sam. 16.)

13. David and Goliath. (1. Sam. 17.)

14. The Wise King Solomon. (1 Kings 3.)

15. Solomon Builds the Temple. (1 Kings 5.)

16. Elijah Fed by the Widow. (1 Kings 17)

17. Naaman the Leper. (2 Kings 5.)

18. Daniel and the Lion's Den. (Dan. 6.)

19. The Birth of Jesus. (Luke 2.)

20. The Angels and the Sheperds. (Luke 2.)

21. The Story of the Wise Men. (Matt. 2.)

22. The Boy Jesus. (Luke 2.)

23. Feeding the Five Thousand. (John 6.)

24. The Good Shepherd. (Luke 15.)

25. Christ Blessing Little Children. (Mark 10.)[37]

These verses contain Bible stories familiar to most Christians and basic to an understanding of Christianity. For example, they tell of Creation, Noah's ark, the story of Moses and the birth of Christ. A close examination of these stories shows,

----

37. "Education Committee Report-Annual Conference 1928," Sanoyea Mission Records.

however, that they reflect the mission's conversion strategies and goals. Five of the stories (11,12,13,22,25) are about children and show what children can do to spread the faith. "The Boy Samuel" tells of a Hebrew prophet to whom God speaks even though he is a child. God warns Samuel that he is going to punish Samuel's father and his descendents because Samuel's father allowed his sons to "blaspheme" God. This clearly parallels to the Kpelle child's own situation in which his family quite likely "blasphemes" by continuing or allowing Kpelle rituals. The story shows that the child himself can become one of God's chosen even if his family does not and warns the child that his family will face divine punishment if they do not also convert. The stories about David's and Jesus' childhoods demonstrate the bravery, wisdom and steadfastness to Christian beliefs which even children can show. They set up models which the children should emulate.

The stories about miracles, that is, demonstrations of God's power, also show the missionaries emphasis on certain themes especially relevant to neophyte Kpelle Christians. Three of the stories (9,16,23) concern miracles in which scarce food is made plentiful. These stories almost certainly struck home to the Kpelle children becasuse periodic hunger was endemic to the Kpelle subsistence economy.[38] In these stories God feeds the hungry much

----

38. The last few weeks before the rice harvest were known as "hungry time" throughout Liberia and the missionaries complained that the lack of food prevented people from thinking about the Gospel. See G.C.

as powerful people- chiefs, lineage elders and patrons- were expected to do in Kpelle society. It is not clear whether the mission intended these stories to be taken literally and that they were committing themselves to feed the hungry. They may have intended for the stories to be metaphors of a "spiritual" hunger. However, in the Kpelle context the stories took on specific, perhaps unintended, meanings.

The other stories of miracles focus on either God's protection of the faithful against overwhelming opponents (8,10,13,18) or on God's ability to heal the sick (16,17.) The "protection of the faithful" theme anticipates that children would face hostility and attempts to prevent their conversion. These stories encouraged them to persevere in the face of social pressure. The healing stories reflect the mission's attempt to replace Kpelle medicines in the treatment of the sick. These demonstrations of God's power showed the medical superiority of Christianity and the mission.

Three of the stories (7,11,14) show the missionaries hope and belief that the children they trained would become the future leaders of the Kpelle. The stories of Moses and Solomon taught that the best leadership came from those who were inspired by God. The anointing of David demonstrated that even the youngest child could demonstrate signs of future leadership and grow up to become an important political figure.

Leonard, "Liberia's 'Hungry Time'" Foreign Missionary, 40 (1920):9-11.

Other stories, usually set in family situations, taught moral values (3,4,5,17.) Jealousy of others, deceit, greed, betrayal of trust, and incorrect behavior towards kinspeople are condemned and either punished or pardoned by a magnanimous gesture. As I shall show below, these themes were also reiterated in pre-baptismal training and attack the Kpelle achievement ethic and big man system. These Bible stories therefore served not only as an introduction to Christianity but also presented themes which expressed the missionaries hopes and goals for the future, their strategies to discredit Kpelle religion as an explanatory and medical treatment systems, and the social exigencies of the conversion process.

The missionaries were more familiar with Bible study than with reading instruction. As a visiting educator remarked about Liberian mission education:

> They have failed to realize that teaching is a profession, the same as medicine and theology, and while they require their clergymen to take special courses of training for the ministry, these same clergymen are turned loose in the classroom to sin against the children! Others send American women over with practically no training, to teach school, and they are making a botch of it. Instead of Africa being the easiest field to work in, it is probably the most difficult, for there are all the complications of a backward people, a different race, religion and social order- coming in contact with all

the forces of modern civilization.[39] Nevertheless, the mission schools were the only educational opportunities open to Sanoyea children.

By the end of 1928 the evangelistic work also began to see some returns. The mission had decided from the beginning that Dagle should concentrate on evangelism rather than the educational program. He began to produce some results.[40] The evangelistic work that had started when the schools were closed, continued once the schools reopened. By 1930 there were 150 baptized Christians in the Sanoyea area, though over half of these were schoolboys and mission workers.[41] Church services were held every Sunday with an average of forty five people attending. Sunday and Wednesday evenings averaged fifty two people present.[42] A 1931 estimate put actual church membership at about thirty with about twenty people attending pre-baptismal classes.[43] Although these numbers seem small they represented a significant increase in the evangelism program. The churches were actively pursuing new members. The three full-time evangelists and two part-time workers managed to reach

----

39. "Letter from Mr. Sibley," THE Foreign Missionary 46,8 (August, 1926) pp.26-29.

40. "Report of Fifth Annual Conference," 1928, p. 3, LCLA.

41. "Sanoyea Congregation Report," (1930) p. 1, LCLA.

42. "Sanoyea Congregation Report." 1928, p. 3 LCLA.

43. M. Edwin Thomas, " A New Day in Liberia," Foreign Missionary 51,5 (1931), 2-4.

seventy one villages in 1930 and to start religious classes in sixteen of them.[44]

Dagle made efforts to draw more of the local people into the evangelical work. He tried to change the organization from one in which outsiders did most of the teaching to one in which closer ties existed between the Christian teacher and the local people. By 1933 the typical Christian worker at Sanoyea was, "a former Sanoyea schoolboy, who has had about a fourth grade education and has come into mission service after being for several years out of touch with the Mission and the Church."[45] These people worked hard for the mission and membership rose.

Dagle had created optimism among the Sanoyea mission workers and among his superiors- the mission administrators at Muhlenberg station in the Americo Liberian settlements. The mission administration held Sanoyea up as a model station, "the most promising field in Liberia." They proudly proclaimed that progress was being made toward "a new day in Liberia."[46] All of this optimism and much of the momentum at Sanoyea came to a crushing halt with Dagle's sudden death from blackwater fever in August, 1933.

----

44. "Sanoyea Congregation Report," (1930) p. 1, LCLA. Unfortunately, this report does not name the villages visited so it is impossible to estimate the population reached.

45. Robert S. Oberley, "Report of Interior Trip - Oct.-Nov., 1933," p. 2, LCLA.

46. M. Edwin Thomas, " A New Day in Liberia."

An examination of Sanoyea station after Dagle's death showed that much of the station's promise had been illusory. Sanoyea had received much publicity in mission publications because it had been self-supporting. Not only had a church been constructed without mission funds, the Sanoyea congregation also paid $200.00 per year as the salary for a teacher in another town.[47] The publicity gave the impression that all members of the congregation tithed, thus creating the necessary funds for these projects. An investigation after Dagle's death revealed that only mission employees tithed. Mission workers only received 90% of their salaries on payday. The other 10% was withheld and put into separate envelopes. As the workers entered church on Sunday they received the envelopes which they placed in the offering baskets themselves. As the report phrases it, "There is no indication that this is done unwillingly, but what the result would be were each worker to be given his salary in full is not known."[48] The investigation also discovered that about half the Sanoyea congregation's income had come from Dagle himself. Church members not supported directly or indirectly by the mission only made slight donations.[49]

----

47. "Sanoyea Station Report," (1930) p. 3 LCLA.

48. Robert S. Oberley, "Report of Interior Trip," p.2,LCLA.

49. Robert S. Oberley, "Report of Interior Trip," LCLA p. 2.

While the Sanoyea station did not live up to the grand expectations of the mission administrators, it had progressed under Dagle. Perhaps Dagle's most important achievement was the creation of a self-sustaining organization which did not fall apart after his death. By 1933 the pattern of evangelist activity had been established and would continue to produce a steady trickle of people undergoing baptism.

The missionaries, evangelists and catechists working the Sanoyea district had set up regular circuits of villages which they visited periodically.[50] When an evangelist first entered a town, he would visit the town chief to ask for permission to hold a church service. The mission workers had established favorable reputations in the area and most villages had people who had some idea of the mission. Most town chiefs were, therefore, willing to allow the church services and would send word around that the evangelist had come. The evangelist generally held service in the evenings and, by lamplight, would set up charts illustrating various Bible stories. He might also circulate small picture cards showing Jesus performing miracles or preaching sermons. After the sermon those interested would remain to begin memorizing the Lord's Prayer or other Bible verses. The evangelist would appoint the person who had made the most progress as leader to drill the people until the evangelist could return. In this way the

----

50. The following account is a composite drawn from interviews with former evangelists R.B. Lowell, Amanda Gardiner, Peter Giddings, and Philip Richards.

evangelist tried to draw people into their own conversion process and to establish the nucleus of a self-sustaining congregation.

On subsequent visits, the evangelist would gradually try to get people to give up their old religion by bringing any charms or other ritual objects to the evangelist for disposal or by throwing them away. The evangelists tried to get the seriously ill to go to Sanoyea dispensary. When the missionaries themselves made the rounds they often brought a victrola to play religious music and attract attention. After several such visits the evangelist would establish regular baptism classes. When the evangelist thought the people had reached the proper level, the missionary would come to the village for final testing and baptism.

Martin Luther's Small Catechism written in 1529 formed the basis for the baptism classes. Luther wrote this catechism for sixteenth century Saxony peasants who had no knowledge of Christian teachings and only a few trained pastors- conditions similar to those in Liberia. Luther felt that ministers should first teach people to memorize Bible texts. Only after rote memorization could they be taught the meaning of those texts.[51] The Lutheran missionaries at Sanoyea accepted this as their educational philosophy and indeed it fit well with the normal Kpelle educational

----

51. Martin Luther, "Luther's Small Catechism," in The Book of Concord trans. and ed. Theodore G. Tappert (Philadelphia: Fortress Press, 1959) p. 338.

procedures.[52] The Small Catechism was written during the Reformation when Luther rebelled against what he called, "the tyranny of the Pope." Luther felt that one could not compel people to accept the sacraments, but must draw people to religion by demonstrating the advantages of accepting it and the disadvantages of rejecting it.[53] The Lutheran missionaries consequently felt that their teachings had to emphasize the blessings of becoming Christians and the horrors facing those who did not convert. This is a thread that ran through their religious instruction and their sermons.

An individual's formal training in Christianity began with the ten commandments. The first three commandments, according to Luther's exegesis, concern the relationship between man and God. The first commandment, "You shall have no other gods," "not only forbids other worship, but also means that serving God should be man's major purpose in life." The second commandment, not to take the Lord's name in vain, not only prohbits cursing and swearing but also was taken to prohibit magic because magic used God's name. Instead of using magic Christians should, "in every time of need call upon Him, pray to Him, praise Him and give Him thanks." [54] The third commandment exhorting

----

52. See John Gay and Michael Cole, The New Mathematics and an Old Culture: A Study of Learning among the Kpelle of Liberia, (New York:Holt Rinehart and Winston, 1967).

53. Martin Luther, "Small Catechism," p. 340

54. Ibid p. 342.

people to keep the Sabbath also meant that people should be willing and eager to hear the preaching of the Word on Sundays.

The rest of the commandments are regulations to prevent conflict within communities.[55] These regulations designed for German agricultural or pastoral communities were also quite applicable to Kpelle village life. These commandments addressed the values appropriate to the kinship based social system and the achievement based "big man" social system discussed in Chapter 1. The commandments to honor thy father and mother, not to kill, and not to bear false witness supported the values of the kinship based system. Before the coming of the Americo Liberians, the Poro Society had upheld these values. For example, the Poro had adjudicated all killings - accidental or intentional - because the spilling of blood was a crime against the ancestors and the earth. The commandments against covetousness indirectly attacked the "big man" system. Envy of "big men" created tensions in Kpelle society which often resulted in witchcraft accusations. At the same time, however, envy of others was one of the major motivations which made the achievement system work. The missionary attack on covetousness was also an attack on ambition and materialism.

Two of the commandments concerned women in Kpelle society. The prohibition against adultery and coveting thy neighbor's wife must have seemed particularly aimed

----

55. Ibid p. 342-3

at the Kpelle. As we have seen disputes over women had been the source of most wars and many court cases among the Kpelle. The ability to take a lover was one of a woman's few means of mitigating her position within the male dominated Kpelle social system. Wealthy men also used adultery fines to gain money or labor and to bind people to them.

The missionaries saw these practices as immoral and did not see how they fit into Kpelle society. They told the people that such behavior was against "the word of God." They concluded this lesson by reminding people that God promised to punish those who did not keep the commandments and reward those who did.[56]

The next stage in the villagers' religious education was the memorization of the Apostles' Creed which sets out the basic theology of Lutheran Christianity. Luther divides the creed into three articles- one on Creation, one Redemption, and one on Sanctification. Each article explains one aspect of the Holy Trinity. The first article emphasizes that God not only created all things, but also sustains and provides for man- his creation. God provides this care not because man merits it, but out of divine love. Man should, therefore, praise, serve and obey God. The second article explains that man cannot come to an understanding of God or Christ on his own, but only through the intervention of the Holy Spirit.[57] As the final stage of their pre-baptismal training, the

----

56. Ibid p.344
57. Ibid p. 344-5

mission taught the Lord's prayer and stressed that prayer rather than ritual was to be the main form of communication between man and God.

Some discussion of these Lutheran doctrines makes it possible to know essentially what version of Christianity was taught in the region. To be sure, the extent to which the above doctrines actually got through to the people of Sanoyea is problematic given the long chains of transmission. The missionaries complained that evangelists had deviated from this model and that the Christian "message" was not taught the same way in all areas.[58] These teachings, however, formed the core of Christian training and the evangelists recognized that few alterations should be made. A standardized teaching program had to wait until the development of educational materials after World War II.

Luther's <u>Small Catechism</u> served as the basis for training before baptism. Once enough people had converted to form a small congregation, the evangelist faced different problems. At this point the crucial problem was to create a strong sense of community among the small group of Christians. One of the first ways to do this was to undertake the common project of raising a building which could be used for classes and church services.[59] Throughout their training people

----

58. Report of the Committee on the Instruction of Luther's Catechism, (1950) Sanoyea Mission Records, Sanoyea (hereafter abbreviated SMR.)

59. Interview with Amanda Gardiner, March 11, 1977.

had been encouraged to help each other and to conduct classes or services even when the evangelist was not present. A strong Christian group made it easier for individuals to resist the social pressures to quit. Non-Christians would jeer at services and try to convince people to remain true to Kpelle religion.

> Should [someone] manifest too great an interest in the mission preaching he would immediately be stamped as a "God-palaver-man" or taunted with jeers from his people that he is no longer a "countryman." He is now a "foreigner" having accepted the civilized "God-palaver." This ridicule becomes so severe and is so unpleasant that few, very few are brave enough to withstand it.[60]

The evangelists therefore tried to foster the independence of the small Christian communities by establishing local hierarchies and delegating authority.

The evangelists also tried to reinforce and strengthen the small Christian communities through their sermons. I do not have any samples of sermons, but a 1927 evangelist report from the Gbolomu mission outpost in Sanoyea District lists the Bible texts used during the month of March.[61] The texts reveal much about the concerns of the evangelist and revolve around

----

60. G.S. Leonard, "Barriers in the Bush," Foreign Missionary 41,2(Feb.,1921): 12-13.

61. See Appendix 2, "Evangelist Report for Gbolomu, March 31, 1927" SMR.

several themes. The texts stress that Christians will ultimately be rewarded, "Then we who are alive, who are left shall be caught up together with them in the clouds to meet the Lord in the air and we shall always be with the Lord." Non-Christians will not receive such heavenly rewards, "He will guard the feet of his faithful ones; but the wicked shall be cut off in darkness." The evangelist emphasized God's strength and told them that God would protect them, "Woe to the wicked! It shall be ill with him, for what his hands have done shall be done to him." The Christian community should band together in the face of opposition, "pray for one another," and those prayers would be effective, "The prayer of a righteous man has great power in its effects."

The Biblical texts used at Gbolomu evoke a picture of the embattled evangelist trying to rally his small congregation. These small congregations faced pressures to give up the new religion and had to be reassured that their sacrifice was worthwhile. The evangelist had to convince them that God was on their side and would provide protection. At the same time the evangelist had to get them to close ranks and support each other. Finally, the evangelist continually emphasized that, despite the problems faced, Christianity was still the only way to get to heaven, "Truly, truly I say to you unless one is born again he cannot see the Kingdom of God." Each individual had to go through the metamorphesis of baptism and conversion. The heavenly reward awaited those who did.

This program of evangelism was in place and operating at the time of Dagle's death in 1933. Small congregations were starting up in several villages, the dispensary continued to do overflow business and the schools continued to operate. Thus on the surface some measurable progress had occurred. Several problems still plagued the mission, however, and would continue to impede its further development. One problem it faced was that of broadening its appeal to all segments of the Kpelle population. School children and mission workers still formed the majority of the Sanoyea church membership. Many adults saw the mission only as an opportunity for children and stayed away.

The mission also had trouble attracting adult males. If one looks only at the adult Sanoyea church members who were not employed by the mission, women outnumbered men two to one.[62] One only has to look at the strict rules the mission tried to enforce for people attending baptism classes to see the causes of this imbalance. A person had to make a public declaration of the intention to become a Christian and to publicly confess all offenses inconsistent with a "good Christian life." The candidate had to demonstrate one year of no more than temperate use of alcohol with total abstinence the desired goal. In the second year the candidate had to make regular contributions to the church and by the third year he must have brought at least one more candidate to the

----

62. "A Good Report from Sanoyea, Liberia," Foreign Missionary 53,5 (1933).

mission.[63] The mission soon found that, "the men seem to have a harder struggle to come and are not as faithful in attendance and abstinence."[64] Women became the first steady candidates for baptism and soon formed the mainstay of the Sanoyea congregation.

Attitudes toward monogamy also help explain this imbalance. The mission insisted that men demonstrate one full year of monogamy before becoming baptismal candidates.[65] The most important men had more than one wife and most of the others saw polygyny as a future goal. Men refused to sever relationships with their wives and abrogate their responsibilities to them. Women, even those in polygynous households, only had one husband and thus were eligible for baptism.

The mission also demanded that people break other kinds of social ties which they felt were inconsistent with the church. For example, the missionaries demanded abstinence from participation in Kpelle rituals. Such abstinence called upon people to forego their responsibilities to family, town and secret society. For example, a boy who became a Christian could no longer perform the ancestor veneration rituals which insured the continuity between the living and the dead. If the boy were an only child, no one would be available to offer sacrifices to his father's spirit after the father's death. Parents would, therefore,

----

63. "Report of the Fifth Annual Conference," (1928) p. 9 LCLA.

64. "Sanoyea Congregation Report," (1930) p. 1 LCLA.

65. "Report of Fifth Annual Conference," 1928.

pressure their children not to become Christians even if they attended the mission school.[66] Some individuals had the responsibility to perform rituals for the family, either nuclear or extended, and kinsmen also exerted pressure to prevent the baptism of these people.[67] Practically all Kpelle rituals were, in some sense, social events and the relevant social groups tried to prevent children and adults from joining the mission and abrogating those reponsibilities.

Converts faced other pressures from the supernatural world as well. Those who believed in the efficacy of the old rituals and the reality of the spirits feared supernatural reprisals for joining the mission. Many feared to be the first to join but were willing to proceed after others demonstrated the safety of conversion.[68] Given these pressures it was not suprising that the church membership was low at the time of Dagle's death. If anything, it is more suprising that they had any members at all. As Chapter 5 will show, these pressures caused many people to alter their religious behavior in ways short of conversion. Only time and changes in mission policy would overcome some of these problems. Until these

----

66. Jennie Larmonth Oberley, "Spirits, Signs and Sacrifices," Foreign Missionary 50,2 (1930): 8

67. Mrs. C.E. Buschman, "Wubu Conversion of an African Chief's Mother," p. 18

68. Mrs. C.E. Buschman, "Native Evangelists in the Far Interior of Liberia, Africa," Foreign Missionary 57,5 (1937):15

problems were solved the flow of new members would remain a trickle.

The work at Sanoyea slowly progressed throughout the 1930's and by 1940 the mission could boast that thirty-two villages contained baptized Christians with several villages having enough Christians to form church organizations. The mission also had to admit that fully half of the villages in the area had not been reached at all and that much work remained even in the villages that they had visited.[69] Yet, the development of African congregations, no matter how small, created optimism among the leaders of the mission. "After many years of seed sowing...[there is] a very marked awakening among the people in the hinterland and a very definite growth in the congregations. Several members are giving their full time witnessing and carrying the light they have received to their own people."[70] The mission hoped that these seed congregations would spread the religion faster and with less cost than the missionaries could.

By 1936 the mission felt strong enough to set up rigid rules regarding the Poro secret society, the central element in Kpelle culture. The mission recommended that in the future non-initiates must promise not to join the society if they were in

----

69. Louis T. Bowers, "Evangelizing the Hinterland," Foreign Missionary 60,12 (1940): 10-12

70. "Report of the Twelfth Annual Conference," (1936) LCLA p. 15.

training as Christian workers.[71] In 1937 the mission decided to "work for the ultimate breakdown of the society by encouraging workers to teach mission children the falsities of their tribal superstitions and by promoting a vigorous internal ferment which will finally explode the bush (Poro) from within."[72] Finally, in 1939 the mission extended its regulations so that all Christians, not just workers and students, faced suspension if they joined the Poro.[73]

The mission's attempts to prevent Christian participation in the Poro ultimately met with failure because the Poro society was too integral a part of Kpelle life. Many people joined the Poro out of fear for its supernatural powers, but many more joined because of its centrality in the social structure. Unless a person joined the secret society he was a man of little account to the Kpelle. He was uneducated, ignorant of the tribal mysteries and not a real Kpelle man.[74] People excluded him from discussions of Poro business, which could be defined very broadly. If he approached people who were discussing Poro matters, they would fall silent and shun him.[75] Such a man was

----

71. Ibid pp. 9-10

72. "Report of Thirteenth Annual Conference," (1937) p. 10, LCLA.

73. "Report of the Fifteenth Annual Conference," (1939) pp. 16-18.LCLA.

74. Interview with Dougba Caramo Carranda, December 29,1976.

75. Interview with Amanda Gardiner, March 3,1977.

not to be trusted for he had not taken the Poro oaths and there was nothing to bind his agreements.[76]

Practical considerations also made Poro membership advisable for Kpelle men. If the Poro masked and costumed leader known as the "country devil" were about, all non-initiates had to hide in their houses so that they would not see him. If a non-initiate saw the country devil, he would be forced to join the society under the penalty of death. To prevent Poro interference with daily routines, the Liberian government had restricted the country devil's public appearances to the night between 9 P.M. and dawn. Non-initiates, therefore, could not travel at night and saw their activities greatly restricted.[77]

The mission plan was also doomed because the Kpelle themselves did not see any contradiction between being Christians and belonging to the Poro. As Peter Giddings expressed it, "Our culture is our culture and our faith is our faith."[78] The missionaries did not make this kind of distinction. To the missionaries, becoming a Christian was to accept Western culture- their own culture- and to reject Kpelle culture. Here the cultural conflict between the mission and the Kpelle becomes clear. What the missionaries viewed as becoming a Christian, the Kpelle saw as renouncing their cultural identity. Whenever the mission forced

----

76. Interview with Dougba Caramo Carranda, December 29,1976.

77. Interview with Amanda Gardiner, March 3, 1977.

78. Interview with Peter Giddings, January 19,1977.

people to make a choice between being a Christian and being Kpelle, it greatly restricted the number of people it could attract.

The mission's prohibitions about participation in Kpelle religious activities led to local political conflicts as well as cultural conflicts, By the late 1930's the mission had grown strong enough to challenge not only the Poro but also the town chief in Sanoyea. The town of Sanoyea had shown little organized opposition to the mission, but tension occasionally occurred between the mission and the town leadership. The most obvious points of dispute concerned town rituals which conflicted with Christianity. On one occasion a townsman had a dream that disease would descend on the town unless certain precautionary rituals were performed. Each household had to furnish a fagot to build a large fire at the entrance to town and to provide rice and palm oil for a community sacrifice. The town chief's representative went from door to door collecting the needed materials. Many of the Christians fled to their outlying farms to avoid the confrontation between their Christian beliefs and their town obligations. Several stayed in the town however and flatly refused to contribute and the town conducted the ritual without them.[79] Although this was only a minor incident, it does illustrate that, by the late 1930's, the Christian element in Sanoyea was strong enough to resist community pressure.

The Liberian government tried to remain neutral

----

79. Interview with Amanda Gardiner, March 3, 1977.

in disputes between the mission and the town, but both the mission and the town chief looked to the government for help. One such dispute concerned a case of smallpox which had resulted in a man's death. The chief refused burial in accordance with Kpelle custom, for the Kpelle believed that if the corpse were buried in Sanoyea soil the disease would remain in Sanoyea. The missionary nurse insisted that the corpse be buried and the chief, upon consultation with ritual specialists, eventually consented to an above ground burial within a termite mound. The nurse rejected this proposal and ordered several mission workers to bury the body in the ground. The chief's men intercepted the mission workers and ordered them not to bury the corpse, but the nurse finally forced the workers to do so. The chief then filed a complaint with the district commissioner- the Liberian government representative- who heard both sides before deciding not to do anything.[80] Although this incident resulted from two differing concepts of disease, it soon became a conflict of authority. That the mission won this round was another sign of its increasing political importance in Sanoyea despite the small size of its congregation.

Until 1938 the Sanoyea station remained under the direction of the nurse in charge of the dispensary. The evangelist staff had continued to open up new villages to missionary activity, but the arrival of Pastor Louis T. Bowers heralded a new surge of expansion. Bowers helped push the mission's expansion

----

80. Karen M. Jensen, "Smallpox in Interior Liberia," <u>Foreign Missionary</u> 55,3 (1935) :9-10.

outside the boundaries of Sanoyea chiefdom for the first time. However, during World War II the growth of the Lutheran mission throughout Liberia slowed down. In 1943 when the Lutherans had some fifteen missionaries and fifty-five African workers, they only managed to baptize one hundred new members in all of Liberia.[81]

World War II had another effect which inadvertently doomed Sanoyea to become a backwater town. When the Liberian government declared war on Germany and joined the Allies in 1944, U.S. Army engineers arrived to help build an airport and roads to aid the war effort. They constructed a road reaching from the airport to the Firestone rubber plantation and beyond into the interior.[82] This road bypassed Sanoyea even though Sanoyea had been located on a major travel route and on all roads proposed by the Liberian government.[83] The road became the major artery into the interior and the towns along the road grew in importance. Totota, a town on the road, boomed in a short period of time and the mission was quick to open a mission station there.

As the mission expanded during the post war period it also began to reexamine some of its

----

81. "Report of the Twenty-first Annual Conference," (1945) p. 2,LCLA.

82. Charles M. Wilson, Liberia: Black Africa in Microcosm (New York:Harper and Row, 1971) p. 172.

83. Luther W. Slifer, "Report on Liberia," (1949) p. 4,LCLA.

policies. By 1946 some missionaries were realizing that they had to bridge the gap between the two cultures - their own and the Kpelle culture - in order to become more popular and reach more people.[84] The old policy of presenting Christianity as the religion of a culture totally separate from Kpelle culture, had proven both unsuccessful and too successful. It was unsuccessful in that only a minority of the people, mostly the young, had been willing to immerse themselves in another culture. This policy had proven too successful in that people who had converted, separated themselves from the people and the culture they had left behind. Conversion therefore had not led to the "snowball" effects necessary for a mass movement.

After World War II the mission began to institute changes to make the church services more appealing and more accessible to the people. Language had long been a barrier with which the mission had to contend. As early as 1913 the mission had commissioned a language study by linguist Diedrich Westermann but the study had not produced the practical material needed by working missionaries. All up-country missionaries underwent some language study upon their arrival, but few had mastered the language. The missionaries conducted their church services in English and had interpreters translate for the congregation. After the war the mission commissioned Dr. William Welmers to work on a Kpelle language course for the missionaries and to

----

84. "Report of the Twenty-second Annual Conference," (1946), p. 33

begin to translate religious materials into Kpelle. Welmers used Sanoyea as his base and completed a thorough study of the language and its dialects.[85] In 1947 his translation of the Lutheran Common Service was used for the first time in the Sanoyea church.[86] From time to time evangelists had done translations of the Lutheran hymns into Kpelle, but in 1949 the Totota mission went even further by using Kpelle Christian songs composed by its members.

The mission also created a literacy program to train the Kpelle to read and write in their own language. The road town of Totota became the center for the literacy program. The mission began to train teachers to go into villages to offer literacy courses. The center developed additional materials for church services and began work on a Kpelle translation of the New Testament, a monumental task that was not completed until the 1950's.[87] With the Kpelle translations of the common service, Kpelle language lessons and Kpelle Bible translations, the mission could begin to standardize its religious instruction. A Lutheran Church investigation of religious instruction showed its shortcomings:

----

85. Welmers' work was published as Spoken Kpelle (N.Y.:Lutheran Church 1950). For a short history of the Lutheran Mission's language programs see Theodore Leidenfrost, "Literacy in Kpelle Land," Foreign Missionary 78,9 (1958): 26

86. "Report of Twenty-fourth Annual Conference,"(1948), p. 9 LCLA.

87. Leidenfrost, "Literacy in Kpelle Land," p. 26.

> The present system of Catechetical instruction is most inadequate, unorganized and very haphazard. Instruction in the different Districts has been very mediocre. Classes are held irregularly and attendance is spasmodic. Evangelists are not well qualified. Length of instruction is much too short. (In some instances instruction [was] completed in less than two months time.) Most instructors begin instruction with the Ten Commandments, spend major part of time covering these, then hastily, in the last few lessons speak about the [Apostles'] Creed and Lord's Prayer, then report their pupils ready for Baptism. Inquirers are then hastily and inadequately examined by Pastor....We also find that all sorts of lessons and courses have been presented, often far removed from the teachings of Luther's <u>Small Catechism</u>. Much of this is due to the fact that our Evangelists and Bible Women are totally unfamiliar with Luther's Catechism and have never been instructed in it.[88]

The mission tried to insure consistency in its teachings by preparing a handbook of Kpelle materials and an instructional manual for its evangelists and religion teachers. These materials reveal what the mission wanted taught, even though the field workers were allowed to change the plans if necessary.

----

88. "Report of the Committee on the Instruction of Luther's Catechism," (1950,) Sanoyea Mission records.

The Lutherans taught that, "The Word of God is a two edged sword. It convicts people of their sin and also confronts them with God's promise of help and salvation."[89] This "two edged sword" was revealed in the first two sermons an evangelist made in a village.[90] The first lesson spoke about Holy God and sinful man," and was based on Romans 1: 15-32:

> For the wrath of God is revealed from heaven against all ungodliness and wickedness of men who by their wickedness suppress the truth. For what can be known about God is plain to them, because God has shown it to them. Ever since the creation of the world his invisible nature, namely, his eternal power and deity, has been clearly perceived in the things that have been made. So they are without excuse; for although they knew God they did not honor him as God or give thanks to him, but they became futile in their thinking and their senseless minds were darkened. Claiming to be wise they became fools, and exchanged the glory of immortal God for images resembling mortal man or birds or animals or reptiles.
>
> Therefore God gave them up in lusts of their hearts to impurity, to the dishonoring of their bodies among themselves, because they

---

89. Manual for Catechists and Evangelists, mimeograph, (1950?), p. B.

90. A complete list of the recommended lessons for evangelists is in Appendix 3.

exchanged the truth about God for a lie and worshiped and served the creature rather than the Creator, who is blessed for ever! Amen.

...And since they did not see fit to acknowledge God, God gave them up to a base mind and to improper conduct. They were filled with all manner of wickedness, evil, covetousness, malice. Full of envy, murder, strife, deceit, malignity, they are gossips, slanderers, haters of God, insolent, haughty, boastful, inventors of evil, disobedient to parents, foolish, faithless, heartless, ruthless. Though they know God's decrees that those who do such things deserve to die, they not only do them but approve those who practice them.[91]

This first evangelization text attacks the Kpelle models of and for reality. The people are condemned for not having honored and worshiped God. By directing their rituals at the nature spirits they had "worshiped and served the creature rather than the Creator." The passage also condemned the darker side of the Kpelle achievement ethic. As we have seen, social approval of the rise of individuals to become "big men" conflicted with the social prescriptions, values and norms of the kinship system. In disapproving of "covetousness," "malice," "envy," "strife," "deceit," "gossips," "slanderers," "disobedience to parents," and

----

91. All Biblical quotes are from the OXFORD ANNOTATED BIBLE, revised standard version, (London: Oxford Univerity Press, 1962).

"ruthlessness," the Lutherans were pointing to those things which the Kpelle acknowledged and criticized themselves. Thus the Lutheran description of Kpelle society struck home.

The evangelist's lesson laid the blame for this state of Kpelle society upon the people themselves. According to the text, the Kpelle were responsible and guilty not only for their own acts but also for approving of the acts of others. Several informants mentioned that the Kpelle did not know they were doing anything wrong in God's sight until the missionaries told them. In this first passage, they were told that this was no excuse and they were still guilty. The idea of responsiblity and guilt was certainly part of Kpelle culture before the missionaries. The idea that their religious behavior was wrong, however, came as a surprise.

> We never had the least idea that we were doing wrong to serve the bananas, trees, water and different other things we called nga mua kweni. We were serving them as our gods. But when the missionaries arrived here they told us that we were doing wrong.[92]

The first text concentrated on the idea of sin; the second text held out the possiblity of redemption through the Lutheran Church:

> For God so loved the world that he gave his only Son, that whoever believes in him should

----

92. Interview with Kekura Gbanakao, April 24, 1977.

> not perish but have eternal life. For God sent the Son into the world not to condemn the world, but that the world might be saved through him. He who believes in him is not condemned; he who does not believe is condemned already, because he has not believed in the name of the only Son of God. And this is the judgment, that the light has come into the world, and men loved darkness rather than light, because their deeds were evil....[93]

The rest of the evangelist's lessons expand upon the themes of sin, guilt and redemption (See Appendix 3.)

Once the evangelist had "opened up" a town, he or she would turn the job over to a catechist who gave more advanced training to those who had become interested. The catechist would organize a six month "inquirers" class for those who wanted to become Christians. These classes expanded on the concepts of God, man and sin, Christ, the Holy Spirit, the Trinity, prayer and baptism. The catechist taught that God not only existed and had created the world, ideas with which the Kpelle were familiar, but also that God took an interest in the world:

> God knows us, and wants us to know Him. That's why He gave us His Bible, so we could learn what God is like, and learn to know

---

93. John 3:16-21.

Him. God holds us responsible for the way we live...God is different from man. He is a Spirit, but not a spirit of a dead person. He is eternal, that is [he] has no beginning or end. He can do all things. He sees and knows everything; we cannot hide anything from Him. Because God can do all things, He can help us. Because he knows and sees all things, he knows and sees what we do. Because he is all wise, He knows the things that are good for us...

God shows his love in Creation. He made all things good and perfect.... God shows His love by taking care of us. He protects us, helps us in sickness and trouble. God shows His great love in His forgiveness which he offers us in Christ Jesus.[94]

The catechist also taught the Lutheran concept of man. Man is inherently sinful and undeserving of God's love. When Adam and Eve were given the choice between good and evil,

> They became sinners. Their sinful nature is passed on to us. Just like we inherit outward appearances from parents so we inherit their sinful nature. That sinful nature causes people not to want God. To love evil instead of good...Man has put himself away from God...Because of our sinful

----

94. "Outline for Inquirers Class," (1950?), Sanoyea Mission Records p. 1.

nature and our sinful life, we are all condemned. We are all slaves to sin, and cannot help but sin.[95]

God has provided a way for man to escape original sin and his inherently sinful nature. Christ lived a perfect life and died to suffer the penalty of man's sin. Those who believed in Christ could overcome sin and escape eternal death:

> Christ suffered death in our place. Death means the separation of the soul from God. Those who believe in Christ will not suffer this eternal death. We are also freed from the fear of death. We need not be afraid of death, if we believe in Christ, because we know he will take us to heaven.[96]

Although the Kpelle certainly believe that people do evil things and things which anger supernatural beings, they did not link the two the way the missionaries did in the concept of original sin. This can be seen in the difficulties the missionaries had in translating the Lutheran concept of sin into Kpelle. The Kpelle believed that all supernatural objects had laws which had to be obeyed in any transaction with them. For example, any medicine would only work if you obeyed the laws relating to it. Mishandling supernatural objects, that is, disobeying their laws was potentially dangerous. The Kpelle also had a word

----

95. Ibid., pp.2, 6.
96. Ibid., p. 5.

for evil deeds- sonyong. The missionary definition of sin joined these two concepts; a literal translation of their Kpelle equivalent is "sin [evil deeds] is any failure to do everything that the law of God requires."[97] Although this cleverly explains sin in Kpelle idioms, it also inadvertently places God in the same category as other supernatural beings when the missionaries were trying to emphasize God's uniqueness.

The missionaries had other problems in fitting the idea of original sin into the Kpelle world view. It was difficult to explain that Adam and Eve sinned because of the devil's temptation, since the Kpelle had no equivalent of the devil in their cosmology.[98] The Americo Liberians had called the masked Poro officials "devils", so that the Kpelle were aware of the word and had formed an equivalent- debele. The missionaries used this equivalent and carefully explained the difference between the Christian devil and the Poro "devil."

Despite the problems of translating these concept into a language where they did not previously exist, the missionaries were successful in introducing the idea of sin into Kpelle culture as the following prayer shows:

> we who are human, we are not clean, we always
> do bad and we are asking you to forgive us

----

97. William Welmers, <u>Spoken Kpelle</u>, Unit 41, p. 3.
98. Interview with Peter Giddings, June 23, 1977.

for our bad ways. Our bad doing caused your son Jesus Christ to die for us and we are asking you to guide us.[99]

This woman had been baptized in the early 1950's and had used the mission's standardized prebaptism instruction material. Her prayer shows that she had internalized the Lutheran concepts of the inherent sinfulness of man and guilt for the crucifiction of Christ. As chapter 1 has shown, the Kpelle world view contained the pessimistic belief that evil people manipulate the spirit world. However, the Kpelle did not believe that all people were inherently evil. For this woman the Lutheran ideas of sin had been successfully grafted onto her Kpelle worldview.

The instructions to the evangelists and catechists show a great concern to differentiate the mission's teachings from Kpelle religious beliefs. They feared that Kpelle would interpret Christian concepts according to Kpelle religious paradigms. For example, they translated the words "soul" and "spirit" by the Kpelle word "moling." "Moling" normally referred to the spirit a person had while alive and which was released after death. The missionaries had to emphasize that the "Holy Spirit" was not the spirit of someone who had once been alive. The missionaries were especially concerned that the rite of baptism not be taken as a magical ritual:

It is not the water...that does the works of

----

99. Interview with Nee Pee, March 18, 1977.

baptism. It is the Word of God which is in and with the water...the water is an outward thing for us to see with the eye.[100]

While the mission struggled to standardize its texts and translate them into Kpelle, it also developed new methods to supplant the piecemeal work of individual evangelists. It instituted a series of evangelistic camps in which a group of mission workers would descend upon a group of villages for three or four days. The mission workers would do intensive evangelical, medical and educational work to create interest in the mission. The mission held three of these camps in the Sanoyea area between December, 1947 and April, 1948. At a typical camp, some twenty Christian workers and medical people reached 3040 people including 501 patients during five days. The mission held twenty church services in eight villages.[101] These "blitzes" were aimed at both attracting new members and renewing the interest of old members much like revival meetings in other parts of the world.

Although the new evangelistic methods were important, the development of an indigenous African Lutheran Church probably had more long run significance than any of the other changes. The Evangelical Lutheran Church in Liberia grew out of the association of African evangelists and Christian workers. The

----

100. Outline for Inquirers class, p. 5

101. "First Convention of the Evangelical Lutheran Church in Liberia," (1948) LCLA.

mission's Liberian staff had met to express grievances against the mission as early as 1924. At that time they had complained about low salaries and asked for more paid vacations just as most workers do. In addition however they complained that they did not participate in the annual conferences which made policy. They also complained about the missionaries' paternalism:

> [We demand] That workers be recognized and treated and addressed as men and women and not as boys and girls. The reason for this is plain.[102]

The workers revived their association in 1943 and voted to hold meetings every two years.[103] In 1947, partly in response to worker demands, the mission incorporated the first Liberian Lutheran Church. The leaders of the Christian Workers Conference formed the nucleus of the new church's officials. The new church had little autonomy at the beginning as the mission still controlled the finances and could veto the church's decisions. The missionaries who headed the mission held important positions in the new church as well.[104]

Despite the lack of real power, the formation of the church was the first step in the mission's

----

102. Christian Workers to Muhlenberg Mission Conference, January 21, 1924, LCLA

103. "Minutes of the Christian Workers Conference," January 16, 1943. LCLA.

104. "Constitution of the Evangelical Lutheran Church in Liberia," (1947) LCLA.

"decolonization" program. Involvement in local political institutions usually comprised the first stage of African political participation in colonized countries. Participation in local church councils began the long process which would eventually lead to African control of the Lutheran church organization in Liberia. These councils consisting of a missionary, local Christian workers or evangelists, and laymen, helped change African participation in church affairs from a passive role to an active one. African Christians received the financial benefits of ties to the American Lutheran churches and received training in church management.

African views gradually became incorporated into church policy while the two institutions- church and mission- coexisted. The African pastors led the fight to reconcile Christianity with Kpelle culture. A 1948 meeting decided, "that those customs in native life not contrary in spirit to the teachings of Christ and dear to the hearts of the people should be retained in Christian life and practice."[105] The report went on to describe those aspects of Kpelle funeral services and marriages which were acceptable. The mission stopped short of allowing polygynous men to join the church but even this barrier would soon fall with the creation of an indigenous Lutheran Church. These developments did not occur overnight, but the elections of African church officers and the ordination of African pastors marked a new stage in the development

----

105. "Report of Twenty-fourth Annual Conference," (1948) p. 26, LCLA.

of the Lutheran presence among the Kpelle.

These changes enhanced the mission's appeal to the Kpelle and contributed to the rapid growth of membership in the late 1940's and the early 1950's. Baptized membership in Sanoyea Church District grew from 193 in 1943 to 749 in 1949 and 1344 by 1954.[106] Much of this growth took place outside of Sanoyea chiefdom itself in the towns of Totota on the main road and Palakwelle- an isolated village in a neighboring chiefdom. Missionaries had first visited Palakwelle in 1939 and the congregation membership there had gone from a mere handful to over 400 in fifteen years. Totota's growth was even more phenomenal, growing from practically nothing in 1947 to over 600 seven years later. Sanoyea's membership also grew but at a much slower rate: from 193 in 1943 to 254 in 1954.[107] The percentage of the district's baptized membership coming from within Sanoyea chiefdom dropped from practically 100% in 1943 to only 19% in 1954. As the mission successfully expanded into the newer areas they concentrated most of their activity there. Sanoyea was being left behind by the other areas and on its way to becoming a backwater of mission activity.

By 1954 the major trends were becoming evident.

----

106. "Sanoyea Chiefdom-Organization 1943" typescript in Sanoyea Mission records: "Second Annual Convention of the Evangelical Lutheran Church in Liberia," (1949) LCLA: "Statistical Survey as of December 31, 1954, Sanoyea District," Sanoyea Mission Records.

107. "Statistical Survey as of December 31, 1954," SMR.

The mission had made important concessions to Kpelle culture, they had organized a local church to provide more African control over local affairs, they had embarked on a literacy campaign, and new areas had succeeded Sanoyea as the most fertile ground for Christianity. Nineteen fifty four, therefore, marks a convenient place to stop and view the period retrospectively as the rest of the decade merely sees the further development of these trends.

One way to evaluate the mission's impact would be to examine the mission's membership statistics and I have indeed used some statistics to chart the mission's progress. Such statistics- particularly from the earlier period- proved difficult to obtain and remain inadequate for any kind of detailed statistical analysis. Moreover, the statistics themselves are misleading and mask certain aspects of events at Sanoyea. The Sanoyea figures, for example, do not show the constant turnover in Sanoyea church membership. In Sanoyea town itself, the church lost 101 of its 158 members between 1952 and 1954, but also gained 53 people in that period. This is a net decrease of 48 people- a significant decrease. It also means that only 57, about one third of the people, remained members during those two years.[108] This turnover results from the high proportion of school children who belonged to the Sanoyea congregation. People from outlying areas came to school at Sanoyea and would leave after graduation to continue their education or

----

108. "Sanoyea District 1952-4," chart in Sanoyea Mission Records.

to find jobs.

Church membership figures are also misleading in other ways. The number of baptized members of the church district is not an accurate indication of how many people are regularly attending church. The number of people taking communion is a better indication of active church participation. Generally only between 35-40% of the baptized members take communion, but occasionally this percentage rises.[109] Although baptized membership dropped from 158 in 1952 to 110 in 1954, communing membership actually rose from 53 to 60.[110] The Sanoyea town church, therefore, had fewer members in 1954 but more active participants.

If one evaluates the mission's impact during the period 1917 to 1954 in terms of baptized church membership, the mission appears to have been an abject failure. Despite thirty-seven years of missionary activity, at no time did more than two or three percent of the Sanoyea chiefdom population become baptized members of the church.[111] Church membership figures alone, however, are not an accurate indication of the mission's influence. Sanoyea proved to be an entry point both into Christianity and into Western culture. Many of the people who joined the Sanoyea church as

----

109. Various "Sanoyea District Council Reports," between 1947 and 1954, SMR.

110. "Sanoyea District 1952-4," SMR.

111. Based on church membership statistics noted above and a population estimate for Sanoyea chiefdom of 14,435 in Paramount Chief to Rev. H. Heilman, January 3, 1946, SMR.

children would later join other churches after they moved away. The school educated thousands of Kpelle children who would not otherwise have learned to read or write. The dispensary treated tens of thousands who would not have received Western medical care. Both the school and the dispensary became parts of Western culture accepted and used by the Kpelle.

An evaluation of the mission should take into account the mission's original goals; to change the culture and religious beliefs of the Kpelle. The missionaries began the period thinking that such changes meant a total transformation for individuals and the acceptance of the whole "package" of Western culture. After World War II they realized that such a transformation would not take place quickly or easily and amended their approach to a tacit acceptance of several aspects of Kpelle culture. They did not, however, make any concessions to Kpelle religious beliefs. A "good" Christian was one who did not practice any Kpelle rituals or use Kpelle medicines. In other words they judged their success by how little Kpelle religion was practiced, not by how much Christianity was accepted. They judged themselves by only looking at the tip of the iceberg, people who had totally converted to Christianity. Any proper evaluation of the Christian impact on Kpelle religion must also look at those who have not converted, yet whose religious beliefs have been affected by the Christian presence. I will, therefore, examine Kpelle religious beliefs to see how Christian beliefs have become part of them.

CHAPTER FIVE

Religious Change in Sanoyea

The religious teachings of the Lutheran Mission had a much wider impact than membership statistics indicate. Although perhaps less than 5% of the population ever joined the church, many more changed their religious behavior in noticeable ways. This chapter will examine which Kpelle religious rituals have changed and which have not. Some of these changes are directly attributable to the mission but in some cases the mission may have been only a catalyst for changes which would have occurred anyway.

Many difficulties arise when examining religious history in small scale societies. It is at times difficult to determine whether religion has changed at all because people try to gloss over change by quickly assimilating new elements into the accepted tradition. The Kpelle concept of God- related to me by several informants- proved to be quite similar to the Christian concept. It was impossible to tell whether the Kpelle had a similar idea of God before the missionaries came or whether they had incorporated Christian ideas into Kpelle religion. Christianity does, however, alter behavior towards God whether or not the concept itself has changed. I have tried to overcome this problem by comparing the religious beliefs of the Sanoyea Kpelle with those of Kpelle in other areas whenever possible.

The individual variation of religious behavior within a society creates a second problem for the historian. In Chapter One I described Kpelle religion as a set of alternatives from which individuals use those elements compatible with their personal experience and goals. Raymond Firth writes, "it is this selective process which results in heresy, apostasy, schism and conversion."[1] This does not mean that an individual's social relationships and associations do not affect the choices that are made. On the contrary, peer pressure, group membership and obligations are very important. However, one should not overemphasize social roles by assuming that they automatically condition religious behavior. Each individual can interpret and respond to his social relations through different kinds of religious behavior.[2]

I also found it difficult to develop a specific chronology for religious changes. Change occurred in different places at different times and usually so gradually that no one could supply specific dates. Moreover, my Kpelle informants tended to see religious change in terms of "the old ways" versus "what is done now." "What is done now" may have originated thirty years in the past though it is not yet fully accepted as part of Kpelle tradition. The opposite error also happens as recent changes presently incorporated into the tradition are projected back into the past. I have tried to provide a chronology by dating events in

----

1. Raymond Firth, "Religion in Social Reality," in Elements of Social Organization, ed. Raymond Firth (Boston, Beacon Press, 1963) p. 246.

2. For a full discussion of these issues see Robert F. Berkhofer Jr., A Behavioral Approach to Historical Analysis, (New York: The Free Press, 1969).

relation to each other so that the sequence of events, if not their specific dates, becomes clearer. If I knew the date at which an informant moved into the Sanoyea area, for example, I would ask about religious behavior when he first arrived. By using key events in the history of Sanoyea and informant biographies, I have been able to piece together a rough chronology.

In this chapter I will first examine the changes in the Kpelle "model of reality"- their explanation of how things work in the real world. Then I will look at changes in the "model for reality"- the system of rituals for coping with the world. I will discuss how rituals and medicines have or have not changed under Christian and Muslim influence. Finally, I look into the sociology of religious change and the problem of choosing a religious identity in a heterogeneous religious community. Heads of families, old people, young people, men, women, laymen and religious practitioners not only have different views of the Kpelle religious system, they have affected and responded to change in different ways. I will try to analyze these differences and how they have contributed to the general pattern of religious change.

The Lutheran mission's goal was to replace the Kpelle model of reality by demonstrating that Kpelle rituals and medicines were ineffective. To the missionaries the Kpelle belief in spirits and witchcraft were superstitions to be replaced by the idea of an omniscient, omnipresent and omnipotent Christian God. The missionaries misinterpreted Kpelle religion as a system of explanations, believing that the Kpelle attributed misfortune, illness and evil to supernatural beings.[3] A few minor evil spirits existed in Kpelle belief, but most spirits were morally neutral though potentially dangerous. For the most part the supernatural entitites were only the agencies for unfortunate occurrences. The ultimate cause of misfortune usually resided in some human activity or failing. The breach of custom, jealousy, ambition, greed or other ill feelings set supernatural forces in motion.[4] The Kpelle explanatory system, therefore, was really based on Kpelle experience of human nature. To discredit it entirely the missionaries would have had to convince the Kpelle not only that the spirits did not exist but also that human nature was fundamentally different.

This can be seen more clearly by looking at witchcraft. Witchcraft- psychic attacks on others- is usually proven by showing that ill feeling exists between the accused and the victim or one of his relatives. Monica Wilson tells of an African who could not believe the whites who insisted that witchcraft did not exist in European society. To that informant this was equivalent to saying that jealousy and ill feeling did not exist in white society.[5] The Kpelle thought about witchcraft in the same way and the mission's

----

3. This attitude is evident in many articles written by missionaries. For example, see F.H. Bloch, "Paganism, New and Old in Liberia," Foreign Missionary 49,5 (1929): 19-21.

4. See Chapter 2 above.

5. Monica Wilson, Religion and the Transformation of Society, (London, Cambridge University Press, 1971), p. 36.

attempt to discredit witchcraft as an explanation never succeeded.

Christian teaching does seem to have changed the Kpelle notion of God. I have already explained that it was difficult to get information about the Kpelle's pre-Christian concept of God although all informants including missionaries insisted that the Kpelle had such a belief.[6] Beryl Bellman, an anthropologist who worked among a different Kpelle group, has raised the intriguing notion that the Kpelle conception of God is so different that researchers have overlooked it. Bellman believes that the Kpelle believed in an immanent God, that is, a God who was part of this world. What some have called animism, the belief that plants, animals, or inanimate objects have spirits, is really the Kpelle belief that God manifests himself in such objects.[7] The Kpelle themselves say that they would worship trees, large rocks or creeks only because "God's name is there."[8] Early Judeo-Christian traditions in the Old Testament contain traces of such a concept. Moses' encounter with the "burning bush" is a well known example. My evidence neither supports nor denies Bellman's speculation, however, the idea is interesting enough to call for further investigation.

----

6. Articles from missionary journals also confirm this belief was present in the past. See F.H. Bloch, "Paganism, New and Old in Liberia," <u>Foreign Missionary</u> 49,5 (1929): 19

7. Private conversation March, 1978 at Stanford University.

8. Interview with Baakoli Zentel, March 22, 1977.

Future investigators should do research in other Kpelle areas that have had less contact with the missionaries and try to do more research into creation myths and other actions specifically attributed to God and the relationships between the nature spirits and God.

The major change in the Kpelle explanatory system has been in the extent to which God was thought to take an interest in the everyday world. All my Kpelle informants agree that before the mission came, people did not pray directly to God. They thought that God was too high above man to listen to human entreaties.[9] The mission taught that God was accessible to man and took an interest in the affairs of men. The Christian God could make moral judgments, punish those who transgressed and reward or protect his favorites.[10]

The idea that God took more of an interest in the world complemented the Kpelle religious explanatory system rather than contradicting it. The new idea that God served as a moral arbiter- meting out punishment and rewards based on human behavior- is consistent with the Kpelle principle that it is human action which initiates supernatural intervention in the everyday world. God's new interest in the world did not deny that jealous, greedy or overly ambitious people could use the lesser spirits to cause misfortune; it simply implied that they risked punishment for their actions. God himself could not be used for such purposes and

----

9. Interview with Amanda Gardner, June 10, 1977.
10. See Chapter 3 for a full discussion.

might indeed foil such supernatural attacks. The expanded role of God in the Christian teachings did not supplant existing beliefs but rather added a new dimension to the Kpelle explanatory system.

A significant change has also occurred in the Kpelle concept of an afterlife. The Kpelle believed that everyone, regardless of what kind of life they had led, lived in "God's town" after death. God's town was separated from the known world by a wide river. A man must struggle to reach God's town.

> When he reaches the waterside he calls the dead people whom he knows. They then come with a canoe across and take him over. But this is not so easy and is dangerous for the soul as the canoe rocks very much and he has to be on steady lookout that he doesn't fall into the water.[11]

If a person with a seemingly fatal illness manages to recover, it is because the dead did not like him and would not agree to cross him. Even if the dead do agree to help a person, that individual must do most of the work in crossing the river because the dead will not talk to him until they reach the other side.[12]

In the Kpelle concept of the afterlife the quality of a man's life had little to do with getting

----

11. H.O. Rohde, "Death in the Kpelle Mind," Muhlenberg Tidings 1,11 (June, 1916): 2, Lutheran Church in Liberia Archive.

12. Ibid., p. 4

into heaven. There are pitfalls attached to making the final crossing, but one achieves it by individual effort not because of the ethical stance one took during life. The Christian concept of heaven differed greatly from the Kpelle notion. According to the missionaries, only Christians who had lived good lives would enter heaven. Non-believers and those believers who had sinned and not been forgiven would enter hell- a concept foreign to Kpelle theology.

The gradual incorporation of the Christian idea of heaven into the Kpelle model of reality greatly increased the mission's ability to change Kpelle religious practices. The missionaries had, in effect, tried two ways to get the Kpelle to convert to Christianity. They first tried to show that Kpelle rituals were ineffectual and should be replaced by the more effective Christian scientific practices.[13] This approach could only have limited results because most religious systems have "fail-safe" mechanisms which enable them to survive failure and ineffectiveness. If a ritual does not bring about the desired result, it can be attributed to an incorrect diagnosis by the diviner, incorrect ritual procedures, unconfessed bad feelings or several other causes. To discredit Kpelle religion because of ineffectiveness is a difficult and long term process because it requires continued failures and rare successes in Kpelle models for reality.

It was quite a different thing to try to

----

13. See Chapter 3.

establish that only Christianity will get one into heaven and this was the missionary thrust that led to more conversion success. Once the Kpelle accepted the Christian concept of heaven the missionaries were in a strong position to press their case. They could then argue that Kpelle ritual displeased God and could keep one out of heaven. Many informants stated that they did not know that they were doing anything wrong until the missionaries told them.[14] Once people accepted that Kpelle rituals were "wrong", there were distinct changes in religious behavior. In Geertz's terms, changes in the model of reality engender changes in the model for reality.

Changes in the explanatory system proved difficult to document and impossible to date except by looking at the changes in religious behavior they caused. Religious behavior among the Kpelle usually takes the form of ritual and rituals can change in several ways. A ritual can simply fall into disuse and disappear or it may continue but be stripped of its supernatural purpose.[15] The throwing of rice at an American wedding is the remnant of a ritual designed to protect the newly married couple from demons. In modern times it has continued as a custom but with no religious content. Such remnants lose their ability to modify behavior when they no longer have a connection

----

14. For example, Interview with Kekura Gbanakao, April 24, 1977.

15. For a South African example see Monica Wilson, <u>Religion and the Transformation of Society</u>, (London: Cambridge University Press, 1971) p. 72.

with the model of reality. In other words when people stop believing that demons are active in the world, or that rice can stymie demons, it is less important to throw rice.

Some rituals will not disappear, yet will continue to be practiced only by a limited segment of the population. As long as someone continues to pass on the esoteric knowledge necessary to perform the ritual, the ritual will remain a part of the religion. If the esoteric knowledge is lost or no successors appear to carry it on, the ritual enters what I call a "grandfather" stage. A "grandfathered" ritual is one which has dropped out of common use and will die out altogether when the current generation of practitioners passes away. Such rituals are on their way to disappearance, however, they could be revived if demand increases and new people learn to perform them.

Rituals can also be modified in either major or minor ways to fit into changing social conditions. The Poro bush school, for example, has changed from a three year course to one which can be completed during a child's three month public school vacation. Modifications can combine elements from different religions as often happens in Kpelle funerals. Christian services can be combined with the addressing of pleas to the corpse not to return- a standard part of Kpelle funeral ritual.[16] Even minor modifications can potentially weaken the authority underlying the

----

16. Paul Counts, "Missionary Work Changes African Burial Customs," Foreign Missionary 47,2 (1927): 22-24.

ritual, for most rituals are based on tradition. Some authority in the past, whether it be ancestors, early Christians, or the Prophet Mohammed, knew the correct procedure and passed it down. Modifications will be accepted if they do not challenge the authority of tradition or if they are supported by some new authority- for example, a prophet or even a missionary. Finally, entirely new rituals can be introduced as was the case with both Christianity and Islam. The acceptance of new rituals, whatever their source, also occurs after the acceptance of the authority from which they are derived.[17]

All four types of ritual change - disappearance, grandfathering, modification and the introduction of new rituals - have occured among the Kpelle of Sanoyea. Regular sacrifice to the spirits in plants, creeks or rock formations has all but disappeared in Sanoyea. All my informants agreed that this ritual is rarely seen in public anymore, although people had to admit the possibility that it was still done in secret.[18] I believe that the slow disappearance of this ritual results from the change in the Kpelle concept of God. As God has assumed more prominence, sacrifices to these spirits have decreased. According to informants, the sacrifices were based either on the belief that these spirits could influence events on their own or because the spirits were used as

----

17. Clifford Geertz, "Religion as a Cultural System," in The Interpretation of Culture, ed. C. Geertz (N.Y.: Basic Books, 1973). pp. 109-110.

18. Interview with James Cooper, April 13, 1977.

intermediaries to God.[19] Insofar as these spirits had powers of their own, they have become ineffective or superfluous when communication with God's greater power is possible. The mission stressed that Christ would serve as man's intermediary with God and that direct prayers would be heard by God.[20] The idea of an accessible God open to prayer has spread far beyond those who call themselves Christian or Muslim. The plant and geographical spirits have, therefore, ceased to be intermediaries as well, and the ritual is disappearing.

Although the disappearance of these rituals took place gradually, in the town of Sanoyea the 1930's seem to have been the decisive decade. Informants who arrived in Sanoyea during this time confirm that people had stopped performing this ritual in public by the last half of the decade.[21] In other parts of the chiefdom the change does not seem to have happened until the 1950's.[22] The 1930's is also the decade in which the "kwi" world was making its presence felt in Sanoyea town. The Firestone rubber plantation was attracting more people into wage labor. The political scandal surrounding the 1930 slavery investigation had caused a reorganization of the Interior Department

----

19. Interview with Amanda Gardner, June 10, 1977.

20. See Chapter 3 above.

21. Interviews with Amanda Gardner, March 11,1977; Momo Kaine, June 4, 1977; Phillip Richards, June 14, 1977; and R.B. Lowell June 18, 1977.

22. Interviews with Alex Mulbah, April 29, 1977 and James Cooper April 13, 1977.

which had raised the stakes in local politics and made literacy an increasingly important skill. The first classes of mission educated schoolchildren had reached adulthood and some had prestigious positions within Sanoyea or in the coastal settlements. By the middle of the decade the mission for the first time felt itself strong enough to challenge important Kpelle religious institutions like the Poro. Sanoyea Christians refused to participate in town rituals aimed at preventing disease from attacking the town. The growing status associated with "kwi" culture and the social pressure exerted by missionaries and Sanoyea Christians, led to the acceptance of religious alternatives to Kpelle ritual. In the smaller villages where these factors did not emerge until later, religious change also occurs later.

I will discuss the interplay between social forces and religious ideas more fully in the conclusion of this chapter because it is crucial to my argument. At this stage I only want to point out that the social forces leading to religious change had reached a turning point by the late 1930's. The plant, creek and other geographical rituals were the first to change because the change was made in a way compatible with the Kpelle model of reality. A second factor, the lack of a social group strongly opposed to the change, can be seen by comparing this change with attempts to alter the ritual connected with the ancestors.

The Kpelle, like many other African groups, believed in the importance of communication with the ancestors. The ancestors were a family's advocates in the supernatural world interceding on their behalf with

God and other spirits. People could communicate with the ancestors through objects ("nga mua") associated with the ancestor while he or she still lived. Sacrifices were made to these objects regularly and on special occasions to ask the ancestors for help to cure illness or sterility. The objects were left in the care of the person appointed to conduct the ritual, usually the lineage head's mother's brother's son or daughter. The missionaries had launched an all out campaign against these rituals in their drive to convert adults to Christianity. They insisted that anyone who wanted to become a Christian must turn the ritual objects over to the mission or destroy them themselves. The mission strategy was to convince people that the objects were ineffective in curing illness and that God disapproved of their use. The missionaries, as guardians of a new means of direct communication with God and as possessors of effective medicines, were in an authoritative position to make such pronouncements. But, they met with strong resistance for they were attacking kinship group solidarity and individuals' sense of reponsibility to family. Many people refused to join the mission because it meant deserting their family and ancestors. When people did begin to convert, the individuals who did not hold responsibility for these rituals were the first to forego them. Even when people who held the ritual objects were persuaded to join the mission they preferred to turn the objects over to someone else rather than destroy them.[23]

----

23. Interview with Vainzeli Kweli, May 10, 1977.

Despite this resistance, these rituals are gradually fading from Sanoyea ritual life among Christians and non-Christians alike. The social forces which have led to the grandfathering of the ritual have not been strong enough to keep it in the mainstream of Kpelle ritual behavior. To explain this, one must look at the dual nature of the ritual; it was both a way to cure certain diseases and a way to communicate with the ancestors. The Kpelle are quite pragmatic about adopting new medicines and new cures are readily accepted if proven effective. The mission dispensary met with immediate and continued acceptance long before Christian and scientific models of reality made any inroads.[24] The Kpelle did not have to accept "germ theory" or reject the belief that the ancestors intervene in their kinsmen's lives in order to recognize the effectiveness of Western medicines. Western medicines have, therefore, largely replaced the ancestor rituals in the early stages of treatment. Ancestor rituals have not been totally eliminated from the Kpelle medical arsenal because they were not totally ineffective. Whether as placebos, cures for psychosomatic illness or simply ways to muster family support for the patient, these rituals did have real effects and continued to be used when other medicines failed.

As with other ritual changes, informants could only provide approximate dates, but this change has apparently begun more recently and has taken place more slowly than the disappearance of the plant and

----

24. Muhlenberg Tidings 3,11 (April, 1921): 2-3, LCLA.

geographic location rituals. Missionaries and evangelists reported that people in Sanoyea town began turning the objects over to them in sizable numbers during the 1940's.[25] In other parts of the chiefdom this change did not occur until the 1950's and 1960's.[26] Increases in the number of objects turned over to the mission do not mean that the ritual itself had disappeared. On the contrary, at the time of my research, 1976-7, some people still maintained the objects and others still thought of them as a medicine of last resort.[27] However, these people are a small minority of the population and most of them are elderly. One elder predicted that the ritual would disappear in his village when he died because no one else had learned to perform it.[28] It proved impossible to ascertain how long the ritual had been in this stage, but the important point is that the ancestor rituals have suffered a different fate from the plant rituals. The importance of the ritual in family groups and the responsibility individuals have felt to maintain it have resulted in the "grandfathering" of the ritual rather than its disappearance.

Fewer performances of the ritual as a cure led to fewer performances as a ritual of family solidarity because for the Kpelle the two aspects were intimately

----

25. Interview with R. B. Lowell, June 18, 1977.

26. Ibid.

27. Interview with James Cooper, April 13, 1977.

28. Interview with Mulbah Gbamokwellie, April 5, 1977.

related. The purpose of the ritual was to ask the ancestors for help and if one needed their aid less frequently, one needed to communicate less frequently.

The decline of this ritual could be related to alterations in family structure brought about by economic changes. The Wilson theory predicts that increased interaction with the wider world will lead to smaller households, more people spending time ouside their home areas, and many economic relationships formed outside family control.[29] As I discussed in Chapter 1, kinship defines economic obligations among the Kpelle. Anthropologist Caroline Bledsoe found that opportunities to earn cash enabled younger people to sever ties with their elders. For example, young people can often pay bridewealth payments without indebting themselves to relatives.[30] It is hard to judge the extent of these changes because perceptions of the situation differ. I did not do a serious study of household size in Sanoyea so I cannot tell whether the changes Bledsoe noted in neighboring Fuama chiefdom are happening in Sanoyea. Several Kpelle elders I talked with complained that family ties were weaker and that the younger generation did not attach as much importance to the extended family. Younger Kpelle I spoke to seemed to chafe under their responsibilities, yet still tried to fulfill them. It will take a full anthropological investigation of actual behavior to

----

29. Monica Wilson, p. 94.

30. Caroline Bledsoe, Women and Marriage in Kpelle Society, (Stanford, California: Stanford University Press, 1980), pp 117-120.

allow a complete assessment of Wilson's hypothesis in the Kpelle case.

The decline of these rituals did not mean that there was less communication with the ancestors, but rather that different avenues of communication had increased in importance. Kpelle religion contained alternative approaches to the ancestors to which many people turned. The Sanoyea Kpelle had also offered sacrifices at the graves of individual ancestors and would talk to their forebearers at these sites. Such visitations did not fall under the mission's prohibitions even though they were based on the same beliefs about ancestor spirits as the "nga mua kweni" rituals. Since grave visitations were acceptable in the missionaries own culture, they raised no opposition to them among the Kpelle. Several informants cite examples of people replacing "nga mua" rituals with visitation.[31]

The Poro secret society- the core of Kpelle religion- is itself a form of communication with the ancestors. Within the Poro the Kpelle can communicate with the village's collective ancestors and the ancestors could communicate their wisdom through the Poro's masked figures. The Poro school served to transmit the teachings of the ancestors which are important for Kpelle survival. Although the Poro in no way replaced the declining rituals, it did provide a method of ancestor communication that was free from missionary interference. As other forms of ancestor

----

31. Interview with Alex Mulbah, April 29, 1977.

communication changed, the Poro stood out as a stable and distinctly Kpelle institution.

The Poro society was able to survive and flourish while making few concessions to Christianity and changing social conditions. Most Kpelle ritual takes place within the Poro grove and is not open to outsiders. I was, therefore, unable to get descriptions of those Poro activities governed by rules of secrecy. Most informants reported that Poro rituals had not changed significantly, although a few commented that things were not done exactly as they were in "the old days."[32] This does not mean that the rituals are stagnant, but that any changes have been minor enough to satisfy village elders that tradition was being continued. The Liberian government has made a few changes in the scheduling of Poro activities. The Poro school session has been shortened dramatically from three years to a "summer session" which takes place during government school vacation. Parents whose children do not attend government school may continue to send their children for as much of the three year period as they want and can afford.[33] The government also restricts public appearances of masked Poro figures to certain times of the day. On the whole government regulation has not weakened the Poro but protected it from missionary interference and opposition.

----

32. Interview with Kekura Nyang, May 3, 1977

33. Interview with Pastor James Vankpana, February 27,1977.

However, there has been a more subtle change in Kpelle attitudes towards the Poro. Although non-initiates still run and hide when masked Poro officials come to town, the trembling and terror which used to accompany such visits seems to have lessened.[34] The very appearance of the Poro figure, the mask, raffia costume and voice (a deep rumble much like that of a giant bullfrog) were designed to emphasize the unearthly nature of the Poro leaders and to inspire fear among the populace. By the 1960's people still feared the very real sanctions which the Poro can impose for breaches of its rules, but the fear of the supernatural which the Poro represents seemed to have dropped away. However, despite minor changes the Poro has been able to maintain its authority.

Medicines- broadly defined as natural substances which can affect events in the real world- have always been the most flexible part of the Kpelle model for reality. New medicines have been tried and ineffective ones have been discarded without raising doubts that effective medicines do indeed exist. The Kpelle have willingly adopted both Christian and Muslim medicines with alacrity. Nearly all Sanoyea people, including Christians and Muslims, have used medicines of one kind or another. Just like people all over the world, the Sanoyea Kpelle were particularly attracted to medicines which promised miracle cures, get rich quick schemes, something for nothing or medicines which sounded too

----

34. Interview with Amanda Gardner, March 3, 1977.

good to be true.[35] The missionaries believed that all Kpelle medicines with supposedly supernatural effects were attempts by confidence men to rob the peole.[36] Certainly some of the medicines were just that, but others were simply medicines that were predicated on the Kpelle model of reality. They were designed to negate the effects of witchcraft or evil spirits and as long as the Kpelle model of reality is not changed these medicines will continue to exist. Indeed, medicines are the one area of Kpelle religion which continues to expand as new uses for medicines are found by the more Westernized sectors of Liberia's population.[37]

Even the missionaries recognized the effectiveness of some of the Kpelle herbal medicines. The nurses at the mission dispensary would call upon native practitioners if all else failed.[38] The mission's official policy in Sanoyea came to be a reluctant acceptance of Kpelle medicines which did not rely on the supernatural and would not harm the patient.[39] The "hair splitting" between supernatural and natural medicines was a missionary distinction not

----

35. For an example of one such confidence game see interview with Nee Kani, July 11, 1977.

36. Dr. C.H. Nielsen, "The Need of Medical Work in Liberia," Foreign Missionary 41,4(1921):15.

37. Interview with Alex Mulbah, April 29, 1977.

38. Interview with Amanda Gardner, March 3,1977.

39. Interview with Bishop Roland Payne, October 22, 1976.

a Kpelle one. Illness could have either natural or supernatural causes or some combinations of the two but medicines were judged on their effectiveness not their nature. The mission's use of Kpelle medicines further reinforced Kpelle faith in all such medicines.

The mission's growing influence in Sanoyea chiefdom did drive the use of some medicines underground. One of the most important kinds of medicines were those used in ritual performances for the benefit of the entire town. In the last chapter I cited an example from the late 1930's in which Sanoyea Christians refused to participate in a ritual to prevent disease from attacking the town. Most of my Sanoyea town informants insisted that few town rituals were performed there after Peter Giddings became paramount chief in 1940.[40] One informant claimed that some rituals were still being held in secret during the 1950's.[41] My investigation suggests that even though medicines and charms no longer line the entrances to Kpelle towns and village, town rituals continue to be performed. In 1977 when I arrived unexpectedly at a small village in Sanoyea chiefdom, people hurriedly cleared away the remains of a town sacrifice, yet later claimed that such rituals no longer take place. The sacrifice that I interrupted was held in public, but at a time when most people were out of the village working on their farms. The fact that such rituals are still performed is as interesting as the fact that people now

----

40. Interview with Amanda Gardner, March 3, 1977.
41. Interview name withheld.

feel they must do once public rituals in seclusion.

Group size seems to be an important variable in the nature and timing of these religious changes. The individual public rituals were the first to change and they either became private or disappeared altogether. With group rituals, as long as small segments of the group still desired the rituals, the ritual would be "grandfathered" as in the case of ancestor object rituals. Group size was important because people were better able to resist outside pressures to discontinue rituals if they had the support of a group. The existence of groups created responsibilities to others and positions of leadership which caused some to continue the rituals despite mission opposition.

All in all, therefore, Christianity has had a rather mixed effect on Kpelle religion during the period from 1918 to 1960. At the end of that period most Kpelle religious beliefs about the interaction between the natural and supernatural worlds remained unchanged. Most Kpelle still believed that supernatural beings, witchcraft and ancestor spirits could affect daily life in important ways. However, the belief had also grown that God takes an interest in the world and that people can communicate directly with God. Many Kpelle had come to accept the idea of a "heaven" which only good Christians could enter. Religious behavior had changed among Kpelle Christians and non-Christians alike. Mission converts attended church services and participated in Christian rituals like baptism, communion and Christian funeral services. Even many who never converted, gradually gave up sacrifices to plant or geographic totems and to objects associated with their ancestors. Medicines no longer lined the entrances to Kpelle towns and villages and those rituals still performed began to be done surreptitiously. Personal medicines continued in use with new ones appearing and new uses developing for old ones.

A simple listing of these changes tells little about how and why they took place. One must go beyond the actual changes in religious behavior to look at what I call the social process of religious change. The religious changes were part of a cultural diffusion which took place within a specific economic and political context. From the beginning of their interaction in 1917 the Sanoyea Kpelle and the missionaries saw their cultures as clearly distinct from each other. The Sanoyea people called themselves the "country" people and called all outsiders "kwi". For a long time the country culture and the "kwi" culture represented different worlds. Behavior appropriate to the "kwi" world was innapropriate or irrelevant to the country world. Some behavior approved or recommended in the country world was discouraged or even ridiculed in the "kwi" world. The mission and the Poro Society each defined the behavior appropriate to the respective cultures. Each side believed that their culture could be kept distinct and uncontaminated by keeping the two institutions apart. Nothing symbolized this as well as the fences built around the Poro groves and the mission grounds in Sanoyea. The government tried to avoid confrontations between the two groups by regulating Poro activities to protect the Poro from mission interference.

Although, as this study shows, the attempt to keep the cultures separate was ultimately futile, the belief that each culture represented a separate world is important in understanding religious change. In some senses the people of Sanoyea lived in as much of a "Manichean world" as any of the colonized people Frantz Fanon writes about.[42] After the "pacification" of the interior in 1917-22 the Sanoyea Kpelle came to recognize the more powerful resources of the Americo Liberian society. The "kwi" culture and its accoutrements came to represent values toward which many Kpelle aspired. After 1930 participation in local politics and in future "kwi" economic activities came to increasingly depend on literacy skills. The mission school came to be the gateway to the "kwi" world and its material benefits.

The realization of the importance of education was a long and slow process. The first mission students were those the Sanoyea chiefs forced to attend school. The people who had been down to the Americo Liberian settlements eventually came back to tell of the advantages of the "kwi" world and the necessity of education in order to profit in that world.[43] The Sanoyea people were still wary of the mission school until the safe return of the first Sanoyea school graduates who had continued their education at the main

----

42. Frantz Fanon, The Wretched of the Earth, (N.Y.: Grove Press, 1968) p. 41.

43. Interviews with James Cooper, April 13, 1977 and Bishop Roland Payne, October 25, 1976.

Lutheran mission stations.[44] After their return, school enrollments steadily rose during the 1930's when the mission served as the entry point into the Americo Liberian world.

Even when the benefits of education were well established, the decision was a difficult one. The Kpelle recognized that they risked "losing" their children to the "kwi" world and culture if they sent them to the mission school. The Sanoyea Muslims particularly feared that their religion- a minority one- would get lost, "[When] you have sent your son to school he will not know you. He will take all the 'civilized' people's ways. He will not even pray as we do in our traditional way."[45] Many Kpelle and most Muslims, therefore, refused to send their children to the school while others made a great personal sacrifice by allowing their children to go.

Although most informants indicated that they had gone to school to get a better life, the material benefits of a mission education were limited.[46] Literacy was becoming a key skill in the new political and economic order but at the time of the great increase in school enrollment there were actually few opportunities open to educated Sanoyea people. Sanoyea was not very close to any industry; the Firestone plantation two days' walk away was the closest, until

----

44. Interview with Peter Giddings, January 19, 1977.
45. Interview with Bangali Donso, May 26, 1977.
46. Interview with James Cooper, April 13, 1977.

the discovery of iron ore in the nearby Bong mountain during the late 1950's. The mission itself provided a few jobs for its graduates as teachers and evangelists. The opening of government run schools in the 1950's created more teaching jobs.

Despite the lack of opportunities, there were enough success stories to keep alive the hope that education was the road to material benefits. One of the first Sanoyea school graduates began as a slave, went to school, got a job at Firestone and eventually acquired a large rubber farm on his own. Some Sanoyea graduates found jobs in Monrovia or other large towns in Liberia. A handful became successful politicians at the provincial and even national levels.[47] The belief in the potential of education rather than its actual benefits lured people into sending their children to the mission school. Once there, the mission inculcated youths with new religious ideas which influenced their religious behavior even if they eventually left the Christian church.

Christianity's attraction went beyond a calculation of potential material benefit. The identification of Christianity with the dominant group in Liberia, the Americo Liberians, gave Christian rituals a prestige that hastened religious change. David Parkin's study of the spread of Islam in Kenya describes what happens when a prestigious foreign culture comes into contact with local religious beliefs. Individuals try to legitimate or reinforce

----

47. Interview with Amanda Gardner, March 3, 1977.

their social position by drawing on the more powerful resources outside their society.[48] In Sanoyea, Christianity- rather than Islam- was the religion of the more powerful "foreign" culture. The "kwi" culture contributed to the spread of Christianity and the retrenchment of public Kpelle ritual performances. People tried to associate themselves with the "kwi" culture and hide their connections with the country culture. Informant after informant stated that by the 1960's people would make fun of anyone who publicly performed many of the old rituals.[49]

If one compares the effects of Islam with those of Christianity in Sanoyea, the overriding importance of Christianity's association with the dominant culture starkly reveals itself. Both world religions arrived in Sanoyea at the same time and conversion to either offered important trade connections and other potential material benefits. Both offered new kinds of medicine and fully developed ritual approaches to the supreme God. Conversion to Islam called for fewer dislocations in Kpelle life than Christian conversion. Even though both religions required renouncing some Kpelle rituals, Christianity required a long catechism training period before conversion and strict monogamy.[50] In contrast Islam allowed polygynous marriages and required little

----

48. David Parkin, "Politics of Ritual Syncretism: Islam among the Non-Muslim Giriama of Kenya," <u>Africa</u> 40,3 (1970)

49. Interview with James Cooper, April 13, 1977.

50. "Report of the Fifth Annual Conference," (1928), p.9, LCLA.

preconversion training. Despite the relative ease of conversion Islam attracted far fewer converts than Christianity.[51] Islam was less attractive because it was the religion of a small, often resented, minority without any political clout within Sanoyea or indeed within Liberia as a whole. Christianity, on the other hand, was the religion of the European missionaries and the Americo Liberian rulers of Liberia and seemed much more appealing to the Kpelle.

Although the "kwi" world was alluring, it was still a world apart- a foreign and forbidding world in some ways. The same people who sent their children to the mission school to become a part of the "kwi" world also felt that they could not become a part of that world themselves.[52] As we have seen in the last chapter, the mission at first had difficulty attracting adult converts. Once people did start converting, whether for material gain, prestige by association or simply religious faith, they still clung to aspects of their own culture. Those who did not convert but were intimidated by Christian pressure to give up some parts of their religion, became more protective of other parts. For both Kpelle groups the Poro Society became an island of "Kpelleness" which demonstrated that someone was, in the words of one informant, "a real Kpelle man."[53] The Poro Society, therefore, did not lessen in importance as the impact of the "kwi" world

----

51. Interview with Bangali Donso, May 26, 1977.
52. Interview with James Cooper, April 13, 1977.
53. Interview with Sackie Nangbora, March 16, 1977.

grew, but assumed an even greater role.

The Poro had always been the foundation of the Kpelle social stratification system, and it continued as a base for a new system which incorporated "kwi" and country culture. Some people chose to live exclusively in one world- either the "kwi" world of Monrovia or the country world of the small villages outside of Sanoyea. Most people, however, tried to develop some kind of "joint citizenship" which enabled them to shuttle back and forth between the two worlds. The "kwi" world had its own system of social status based on family connections, education and church membership while the Poro and related secret societies formed the basis for country status.[54] Education or success in the "kwi" world carried some prestige in the country world, but anyone who wanted to raise his status had to rise in both the "kwi" and country social hierarchies. President Tubman himself recognized this and had himself proclaimed the head of all the Poro Societies in Liberia in order to solidify his leadership with the country people. On the local level Sanoyea politicians also felt that they must confirm their status; a "big man", had to make sure his credentials were in order in both worlds.

The desire of both Kpelle Christians and non-Christians to hold on to their own culture and the Poro Society's importance in the social stratification system help explain a paradoxical event in Sanoyea's

----

54. See J. Gus Liebenow, Liberia; The Evolution of Privilege, (Ithaca N.Y.: Cornell University Press, 1969).

history. Sanoyea grew from a backwater village to an important town because it was located on trade routes and became a base for the mission and the Liberian government. It did not have its own Poro grove until the early 1950's when the local chiefs were educated Christians and the mission was at the height of its powers. If one were limited to a unilinear theory of religious change- like the Wilson-Horton theories- in which people always move from the polytheistic "traditional" religion to a more "modern" monotheistic religion, then the expansion of the Poro to Sanoyea would form a "reversion." Once the importance of the Poro to the Kpelle ethnic identity and local hierarchy becomes clear, one can understand why both the Christian Kpelle elite and the general Kpelle populace desired to bring the Poro to Sanoyea. Sanoyea had grown because of its connections with the "kwi" world, but it needed its own Poro grove to become a "real Kpelle town" just as much as its population needed the Poro to confirm their own Kpelle identity. The acquisition of a Poro grove under the initiative of Peter Giddings, raised Sanoyea's status in the eyes of the Kpelle, increased the popularity of the leaders, and gave the leadership control of a Kpelle social hierarchy. Far from a reversion, the arrival of the Poro was the culmination of Sanoyea's rise from village to a legitimately Kpelle chiefdom capital.

So far I have looked at religious change among the population as an aggregate, however, the concept of "two worlds" also helps in understanding the reactions of different segments of the population to Christianity. Even though the "kwi" and country worlds each had its advantages, the mission's restrictions forced people to forego things in one world in order to participate in the other. For example, the mission insisted that all converts be monogamous. A man who had achieved some status among the Kpelle would likely have more than one wife as a sign of his wealth and social standing. Such a man could not become a Christian unless he renounced all wives but one. Similarly, if a Kpelle in the mission's employ were found to have more than one wife he would be forced to give up any position he had gained. These restrictions did not apply to secular positions in the "kwi" world directly, but people trying to "make it" in the "kwi" world did try to live according to the mission's behavioral norms.

If one examines an individuals' reaction to Christianity in terms of their potential gains and losses, one can understand why children and adult women constituted the bulk of mission converts. Children, the people who have not yet achieved any status within the Kpelle social system, have the least to lose and potentially the most to gain by converting to Christianity. They will enter the "kwi" world at an early age and receive the most training in the skills needed in that world. Parents will allow their children to convert because of the long-term benefits mentioned above.

Adult women hold relatively few high status positions among the Kpelle and most of these lie within the Sande society- the female counterpart of the Poro Society. There were fewer of these positions and they had lower status than the men's positions. Women also had fewer informal associations outside their daily household routines. Lutheran Church activities provided a social outlet for women and a new, though limited, source of status within the church's lay hierarchies. Conversion did not present as much of a problem for women as it did for men because women usually had less to give up in the country world.

The church also offered women a way to establish their independence from the Kpelle male hierarchy. As the first chapter discussed men held most rights over women. A woman's rights to land and labor usually came through her husband. The Poro's control over the Sande Society and the elders' control over bridewealth regulated marriage patterns in Kpelle society. Jobs as evangelists gave women resources which were not controlled by Kpelle males. Their salaries and mission connections enabled them to accumulate labor and own land. If they so desired, they could more easily obtain a divorce by repaying bridewealth.

Adult men were the ones most likely to be attracted by the mission's "kwi" prestige and to try to use the mission to immediately enhance their own status. Not all Sanoyea Kpelle men sought to acquire status in the "kwi" world, but for those who did the mission's norms defined proper public behavior. The object for people who wanted status in both worlds was to minimize the losses of status in the country world while trying to establish status in the "kwi" world. Adult males' attraction to Christianity shows up in modification of their religious behavior rather than in full scale conversion. Conversion called for giving up too much of their achieved status in the country world:

wives, ritual positions, and Poro offices. Men were more likely to try to make themselves acceptable to both worlds by ceasing to perform some Kpelle rituals publicly while continuing to practice others secretly.

The "two world" hypothesis, therefore, helps us to understand the course of religious change in Sanoyea. As we have seen, each world had its advantages- the potential material benefits and prestige of the "kwi" world on the one hand, and the familiarity and ethnic identity of the country world. The mission and the Poro Society set the norms for proper behavior- especially religious behavior- in each world respectively. The mission and Poro religious norms conflicted as long as each group tried to maintain totally separate worlds. The history of Sanoyea has shown how the "kwi" world slowly emerged as the dominant normative mode of public behavior so that the mission's ideas of proper public religious behavior also came to dominate Sanoyea. Kpelle religious behavior continued but had to be done privately, surreptitiously or within the Poro Society's veil of secrecy. The Poro itself survived because it was so central to Kpelle ethnic identity that the "kwi" world had to accept it. First the Liberian government, then the mission, had to work out a "modus vivendi" with the Poro in order to establish themselves within Sanoyea.

By the 1950's the mission was making some concessions to Kpelle culture by allowing, though not condoning, polygyny and using Kpelle language church services and hymns. Government schools also opened up in Sanoya providing a new "gateway" to the "kwi" world which did not require the adoption of Christianity.

The government schools did not immediately replace the mission school, but they did provide an alternative that became more popular as time went on. These changes have made it easier to achieve status in both systems at the same time by decreasing what one had to give up to make it in the "kwi" world. By the end of the period under study, therefore, the two worlds had become a little less separate. However, as long as Liberia's social structure maintains the distinction between "kwi" and country, religion will reflect this distinction to some extent.

The Sanoyea case study shows how the course of religious change depends on the social and political context in which change occurs. I have argued that choices about religious behavior and affiliation are to varying degrees social choices. Those who choose to convert had to balance their personal convictions with their family and community responsibilities. Conversion therefore varied among different segments of the population according to social position. Even those who did not convert adjusted their religious practices to avoid ridicule and to conform to increasingly "kwi" behavioral norms.

I want to emphasize that my sociological perspective does not discount such intangibles of religious decisions as faith nor does it imply that all religious choices are cold calculations of potential gain. I merely want to point out that, whatever the motives for religious change, there were social consequences and implications in choosing one's religious affiliation. Individuals may have assigned different weights to these implications in making their decisions, but most people took them into consideration.

A sociology of religious change does not tell the entire story. The doctrinal and ideological bases of religion also shape the nature, pace and extent of religious change. The Kpelle accepted those aspects of a foreign religion which fit the perceived structural gaps of Kpelle religion. As I have shown Kpelle religion contained few ritual approaches to the supreme God because Kpelle addressed formal religious communication through intermediaries. The missionaries successfully introduced the idea of an accessible supreme God into Kpelle religion even among those who never converted to Christianity.

To understand Christianity's doctrinal attractions, one must look at the doctrines actually promulgated. Whatever the doctrines formulated by theologians, the Christianity spread in Africa was dependent on the "man on the spot." Even though the mission relied on doctrines formed by its parent church, the missionaries and African evangelists could subtly change Christianity's "message" consciously or unconsciously with subtle shifts of emphasis, deletions and differing translations. The field texts and experiences of the evangelists are therefore the best sources. I have used the mission texts to show how the missionaries tried to convert people and how the messages contained in the texts conflicted or fit into the Kpelle world view. I believe we need more of that kind of analysis to understand conversion.

We need therefore to examine religious change as

both a social and intellectual process. These two perspectives, so seemingly at odds in the past literature of African religion, are really only two views of the same animal. Only by considering both can we turn our sketches of religious change into a full portrait.

APPENDIX ONE

List of Informants

Name	Place	Date
Corinne Allison	Sanoyea	Mar. 8, 1977
Benjamin Barclay	Kilibe	April 5, 1977
Frederick Barclay	Kilibe	April 5, 1977.
Dougba C. Carranda	Brewerville	Dec. 29, 1976
James Cooper	Boye	April 13, 1977
Mulbah Dangolu	Zolita	May 3, 1977
Bangali Donso	Sanoyea	May 26, 1977
"	"	June 10, 1977
Vani Donso	"	May 31, 1977
Amanda Gardiner	Kpona Winni Ta	March 3, 1977
"	"	March 11, 1977
"	"	June 10, 1977
Mulbah Gbamokweli	Kilibe	April 5, 1977
Kekura Gbanakao	Gbanga Gilengta	April 24, 1977
Flumo Gbodai	Gbolomu	March 22, 1977
Moses Giddings	Sanoyea	May 28, 1977
Peter Giddings	Sanoyea	January 19, 1977
"	"	January 27, 1977
"	"	June 23, 1977
Edward Gouto	Monrovia	October 27, 1977
Benda Gwiningali	Gbotoloma	April 26, 1977
Momo Kaine	Sanoyea	June 4, 1977
Nee Kani	Monrovia	July 11, 1977
Mulaba Keita	Sanoyea	May 31, 1977
"	"	June 22, 1977
Vainzeli Kweli	Kilibe	May 10, 1977
D.B. Livingstone	Sanoyea	June 14, 1977
R.B. Lowell	Sanoyea	June 18, 1977
Alexander Mulbah	Sanoyea	April 29, 1977
Sacki Nangbora	Sanoyea	March 16, 1977
Kekura Nyang	Zolita	May 3, 1977
Roland Payne	Sinkor	October 22, 1976
"	"	October 25, 1976
Nee Pee	Sanoyea	March 18, 1977
Joshua K. Raynes	Sanoyea	June 6, 1977
Phillip Richards	Sanoyea	June 14, 1977
James Vankpana	Sanoyea	Feb. 27, 1977
Charles Wellington	Boye	April 21, 1977
Mulbah Wuto	Boye	April 21, 1977
Baakweli Zentei	Gbolomu	March 22, 1977

APPENDIX TWO

Evangelistic Report for Gbolomu, March 31, 1927

Gbolomu, March 2, attendance 21

> Luke 10:16 - He who hears you hears me and he who rejects you rejects me and he who rejects me rejects him who sent me.

Kilibe, March 3, attendance 43

> Luke 14:27 - He who does not bear his own cross and come after me cannot be my disciple.

Vangalai, March 4, attendance 22

> 1 Sam. 2:9 - He will guard the feet of his faithful ones; but the wicked shall be cut off in darkness, for not by might shall a man prevail.

Gbolomu, March 6, attendance 19

> 1 Pet. 5:5 - Likewise you that are younger be subject to the elders. Clothe yourselves all of you, with humility toward one another, for God opposes the proud but gives grace to the humble.

Koblata, March 8, attendance 8

> Luke 18:13 - The tax collector, standing far off would not even lift up his eyes to heaven, but beat his breast saying, "God be merciful to me a sinner."

Kilibe, March 9, attendance 96

> 1 John 1:7 - But if we walk in the light, as he is in the light, we have fellowship with one another and the blood of Jesus his son cleanses us from all sin.

Gbolomu, March 10, attendance 18

> James 5:16 - Therefore confess your sins to one another, and pray for one another, that you may be healed. The prayer of a righteous man has

great power in its effects.

Vangalai, March 11, attendance 24

    1 Thess. 5:16 - Rejoice always.

Gbolumu, March 13, attendance 25

    Psa. 31:15 - My times are in thy hand; deliver me from the hand of my enemies and persecutors.

Forakaliah, March 14, attendance 6

    Psa. 9:10 - And those who know thy name put their trust in thee, for thou O Lord has not forsaken those who seek thee.

Kilibe, March 15, attendance 86

    John, 3:3 - Truly, truly I say to you unless one is born anew he cannot see the kingdom of God. (Nicodemus - baptism)

Gbolomu, March 16, attendance 19

    Psa. 25:4 - Make me to know thy ways, O Lord teach me thy paths.

Bononkalih, March 17, attendance 56

    Matt. 5:7 - Blessed are the merciful for they shall obtain mercy.

Vangalaih, March 18, attendance 19

    Eph. 4:32 - Be kind to one another, tenderhearted, forgiving one another, as God in Christ forgave you.

Gbolomu, March 20, attendance 17

    Isa. 3:11 - Woe to the wicked! It shall be ill with him, for what his hands have done shall be done to him.

Koblata, March 21, attendance 6

    Psalm 61:1 - Hear my cry O Lord, listen to

my prayer.

Kilibe, March 22, attendance 19

>Psalm 119:115 - Depart from me, you evil doers that I may keep the commandments of my God.

Gbolomu, March 23, attendance 20

>1 Thess. 4:17 - Then we who are alive, who are left, shall be caught up together with them in the clouds to meet the Lord in the air and we shall always be with the Lord.

Vangalaih, March 24, attendance 11

>Exodus 20:3 - You shall have no other gods before me.

Bononkalih, March 25, attendance 40

>James 5:16 - Therefore confess your sins to one another and pray for one another that you may be healed. The prayer of a righteous man has great power in its effects.

Gbolomu, March 27, attendance 22

>Exodus 20:8 - Remember the Sabbath day to keep it holy.

Kablata, March 28, attendance 4

>Joshua 4:13 - When the priests who bear the ark of the covenant stand in the river Jordan, it will stop flowing and the waters from above will stand in one heap.

Kilibe, March 29, attendance 18

>Mark 13:14 - But when you see the desolating sacrilege set up where it ought to be... let those who are in Jordan flee to the mountains.

Gbolomu, March 30, attendance 16

>1 Thess. 5:17 - Pray constantly.

Vangalaih, March 31, attendance 14

    I Peter 3:12- For the eyes of the Lord are upon the righteous and his ears are open to their prayers. But the face of the Lord is against those who do evil.
holy.

APPENDIX THREE

Twenty-six Lessons for Evangelists

Topic	Scripture
Holy God and Sinful Man	Rom. 1:15-32
The Promise of Salvation	John 3:16-21, Gen. 3:15
Jesus Christ, God's Son	Matt. 3:13-17, 17:1-13
Jesus Christ, Our Lord	Phil 2:5-11
Christ's Healing Power	John 4:46-54
Christ's Saving Power	Matt. 9:1-8
Conviction of Sin	Rom. 2:1-23, 3:10-26
Christ's Power Over Death	John 11:1-46
The Great Invitation	Matt. 22:1-14
The Parable of the Soils	Luke 8:4-15
Confession of Guilt	Luke 15:11-24
The Kingdom of Heaven	Matt. 13:44-50
The Love of God	John 10:11-16
The Will of God	Matt. 5:13-48
Our Savior's Death	Luke 23:33-49
Repentance	Luke 22:55-62
Redemption	II Cor. 5:17-21, Isaiah 53:3-12
Our Lord's Resurrection	John 20:1-18
Eternal Life	I Cor. 15:1-58
Conversion	Luke 19:1-10, Acts 9:1-18
Faith	Hebrews 11:1-26
Baptism	Acts 8:5-40
Regeneration: the New Man	John 3:1-15
Consecration	Rom. 12:1-21
Christian Growth	John 15:5-11
The Return of Christ	Matt. 25:31-46

SELECTED BIBLIOGRAPHY

Archival Material

Republic of Liberia Archive, Monrovia

>Executive Mansion Correspondence 1894-96
Executive Mansion Correspondence 1896-99
Executive Mansion Correspondence 1905-12
Executive Mansion Correspondence 1910-12
Executive Mansion Correspondence 1920-25
Executive Mansion Correspondence 1924-29
State Department to Interior Department, 1912
Executive Mansion to Interior Department, 1924-39
Interior Department to Department of State, 1926
Interior Department to Executive Mansion, 1931
Interior Department to Department of State, 1934
Executive Mansion to Interior Department, 1939

Lutheran Church in Liberia Archive, Sinkor, Liberia

>Letters to the Board of Foreign Missions, 1922-23 1928-40, 1946-.
Letters from the Board of Foreign Missions, 1922-23, 1929-38, 1946-
Conference Minutes of the Lutheran Mission
  Semi-annual Conferences July,1919-July, 1923
  Annual Conferences 1924, 1926-1948
  Biennial Conferences 1950-1964
Minutes of the Biennial Conference of the Evangelical Lutheran Church in Liberia 1947-51, 1961
Minutes of the Executive Council of the Lutheran Mission in Liberia 1923-
Minutes of the Executive Committee of the

Evangelical Lutheran Church in Liberia
1947-
Miscellaneous Documents 1922-

Works about Liberia

Akpan, Monday Benson. "The African Policy of the Liberian Settlers, 1841 - 1932; A Study of the Native Policy of a non colonial power." Ph D.dissertation, University of Ibadan, 1972.

_____. "Black Imperialism: Americo-Liberian Rule over the African Peoples of Liberia, 1841-1964." Canadian Journal of African Studies 7,2 (1973) 217-226

_____. "The Liberian Economy in the 19th Century; The State of Agriculture and Commerce." LiberianStudies Journal 6 (1975).

Alexander, Archibald. A History of Colonization on the Western Coast of Africa. Philadelphia: W.S. Martien, 1846.

American Colonization Society. Annual Report, 93 vols. New York: Negro Universities Press,

Anderson, Benjamin K. Narrative of a Journey to Musahdu, the Capital of the Western Mandingoes, 1870 and Narrative of the Expedition Dispatched to Musahdu by the Liberian Government in 1874. London: Frank Cass Ltd.,1971.

Bellman, Beryl. Village of Curers and Assassins. The Hague: Mouton Press, 1975.

Blanchard, David G. "The Impact of External
    Domination on the Liberian Mano Economy."
    Ph D. dissertation, Indiana University, 1973

Bledsoe, Caroline. Women and Marriage in Kpelle
    Society. Stanford: Stanford University Press,
    1980.

Bosman, William. A New and Accurate Description of
    the Coast of Guinea. London: Frank Cass Ltd.,
    1967.

Brown, George D. "History of the Protestant Episcopal
    Mission in Liberia up to 1838." Historical
    Magazine of the Protestant Episcopal Church
    39,1 (March, 1970.)

Brown, George W. The Economic History of Liberia.
    Washington D.C. Associated Publishers, 1941.

Buell, Raymond L. A Century of Survival, 1847-1947.
    Philadelphia:University of Pennsylvania Press,
    1947.

Cason, John W. "The Growth of the Church in the
    Liberian Environment." Ph D. dissertation,
    Columbia University, 1962.

Christiansen, Robert; Gay, John; Tamba, Sylvester;
    Brown, Isaac. "The Near Edge of Change."
    Liberian Studies Journal 4,2 (1973.)

D'Azevedo, Warren L. "The Setting of Gola Society
    and Culture: Some Theoretical Implications
    of Variation in Time and Space." Kroeber
    Anthropological Society Papers no. 21
    Berkeley: University of California Press,
    1959.

_____."Uses of the Past in Gola Discourse."
    Journal of African History 3 (1962)
    11-34

_____. " A Tribal Reaction to Nationalism,"
    Liberian Studies Journal, 1,2 (1969):
    2,1 (1969.)

_____ "Tribe and Chiefdom on the Windward
    Coast," Rural Africana 15 (1971.)

Earthy, E. Dora, "The Impact of Mohammedanism on Paganism in the Liberian Hinterland," International Review of the History of Religion 2,3 (1955.)

Fahey, Richard P. "The Poro as a System of Judicial Administration in Northwest Liberia," African Law Studies 4 (1971.)

Frankel, Merran. Tribe and Class in Monrovia. London: Oxford University Press, 1964.

Fulton, Richard M. "The Kpelle of Liberia: A Study of Political Change in the Liberian Interior," Ph D. dissertation University of Connecticut (1969.)

_____ "The Kpelle Traditional Political System," Liberian Studies Journal 1,1 (1968.)

_____ "The Political Structure and Functions of the Poro in Kpelle Society," American Anthropologist 74 (1972.)

Gay, John and Cole, Michael. The New Mathematics and an Old Culture; A Study of Learning Among the Kpelle of Liberia. New York: Holt Rinehart and Winston, 1967.

Gibbs, James L. "Poro Values and Courtroom Procedures in a Kpelle Chiefdom," Southwestern Journal of Anthropology, 18 (1962.)

_____ "Marital Instability among the Kpelle: Toward a Theory of Epainogamy." American Anthropologist 65 (1963.)

_____ The Kpelle Moot: A Therapeutic Model for the Informal Settlement of Disputes." Africa 33 (1963.)

_____ "The Kpelle of Liberia." in Gibbs, James L. ed. Peoples of Africa. New York: Holt, Rinehart and Winston, 1965.

Harley, George W. "Notes on the Poro in Liberia." Papers of the Peabody Museum of American

Archaeology and Ethnography 19 (1941.)

Henries, Richard and Henries, Doris. Liberia: The West Africa Republic. New York: Hermann Jaffe, 1958.

Holsoe, Svend E. "The Cassava-Leaf People: An Ethnohistorical Study of the Vai People with a Particular Emphasis on the Tewo Chiefdom." Ph D. dissertation, Boston University 1967.

_____ "The Condo Confederation in Western Liberia." Liberian Historical Review 3,1 (1966.)

Holt, Dean A. "Changing Strategies Initiated by the Protestant Episcopal Church in Liberia from 1836-1950." Ph D. dissertation Boston University, 1970.

Huberich, Charles H. The Political and Legislative History of Liberia. New York: Central Book Company, 1947.

Jones, Hannah A. "The Struggle fo Political and Cultural Unification in Liberia." Ph D. dissertation, Northwestern University, 1961/2.

Johnston, Harry. Liberia. London: Hutchinson & Company, 1906.

Liebenow, J. Gus. Liberia; The Evolution of Privilege. Ithaca, M.Y.: Cornell University Press, 1969.

Marinelli, Lawrence. The New Liberia; A Historical and Political Survey. New York: Frederick Praeger, 1964.

Moore, Bai T. Tribes of the Western Province and the Denwoin People. Monrovia: Interior Department, Republic of Liberia. 1955.

Nolan, Jay Hamilton. "Culture and Psychosis among the Loma Tribe of Liberia." Ph D. dissertation, Stanford University 1971/72.

Orr, Kenneth G. "Field Notes on Medical Practices in

Central Liberia." *Liberian Studies Journal* 1,1 (1968.)

Ross, Timothy T. "A Preliminary Study of Medical Practices in Two Kpelle Traditional Communities." *Liberian Studies Journal* 5,1 (1967.)

Schulz, Willi. *A New Geography of Liberia*. London: Longman Group Ltd., 1973.

Scott, Anna M. *Day Dawn in Africa or Progress of the Protestant Episcopal Mission at Cape Palmas*. New York: Protestant Episcopal Society for the Promotion of Evangelical Knowledge, 1858.

Shick, Tom. *Behold the Promised Land*. Baltimore: Johns Hopkins University Press, 1980.

Sibley, James L. and Westermann, Diedrich. *Liberia Old and New*. Garden City, N.Y.: Doubleday and Company, 1928.

Staudenraus, P.J. *The African Colonization Movement 1816-1865*. New York: Columbia University Press.

Strong, Richard P. ed. *The African Republic of Liberia and the Belgian Congo: Harvard African Expedition 1926-27*. Cambridge, Mass.: Harvard University Press, 1930.

Sundiata, I.K. *Black Scandal, America and the Liberian Labor Crisis, 1929-1936*. Philadelphia: Institute for the Study of Human Issues, 1980.

Welmers, William. "Secret Medicines, Magic and Rites of the Kpelle Tribe of Liberia." *Southwestern Journal of Anthropology* 5 (1949).

Wilson, Charles M. *Liberia: Black Africa in Microcosm*. N.Y. Harper Row, 1971.

Wintrob, Ronald M. "Sexual Guilt and Culturally Sanctionned Delusions in Liberia." *American Journal of Psychiatry*, 125 (1968.)

_____ "Mammywater: Folk Beliefs and Psychotic Elaborations in Liberia," *Canadian Psychiatric Association Journal* 15 (1970.)

General Works

Ajayi, J.F. Ade. *Christian Missions in Nigeria 1841-1891; The Making of a New Elite.* Evanston: Northwestern University Press, 1965.

Beidelman, Thomas O. "Social Theory and the Study of Christian Missions." *Africa* 44 (1974.)

_____ *W. Robertson Smith and the Sociological Study of Religion.* Chicago: University of Chicago Press, 1974.

Berger, Peter L. *The Sacred Canopy.* Garden City, N.Y.: Doubleday and Company, 1969.

Berkhofer, Robert F. *A Behavioral Approach to Historical Analysis.* N.Y.: The Free Press, 1969.

Bhebe, Ngwabi. *Christianity and Traditional Religion in Western Zimbabwe 1859-1923.* London: Longman Group Ltd., 1979.

Durkheim, Emile. *The Elementary Forms of the Religious Life.* N.Y.: The Free Press, 1965.

Evans-Pritchard, E.E. *Witchcraft among the Azande.* London: Oxford University Press, 1937.

_____ *Theories of Primitive Religion.* London: Oxford University Press, 1965.

Fanon, Frantz. *The Wretched of the Earth*. N.Y.: Grove Press, 1968.

Firth, Raymond. "Religion in Social Reality." in Firth, Raymond ed. *Elements of Social Organization*. Boston: Beacon Press, 1963.

Fisher, Humphrey. "Conversion Reconsidered: Some Historical Aspects of Religious Conversion in Black Africa." *Africa* 43 (1973.)

Fustel de Coulange, Numa Denys. *The Ancient City*. Garden City, N.Y.:Doubleday and Company, n.d.

Geertz, Clifford. "Religion as a Cultural System." in Banton, Michael. ed. *Anthropological Approaches to the Study of Religion*. London: Tavistock Publications, 1966.

Geertz, Hildreth and Thomas, Keith. "An Anthropology of Religion and Magic." *Journal of Interdisciplinary History* 6 (1975): 71-89.

Horton, Robin. "African Traditional Thought and Western Science." *Africa* 37 (1967.)

_____. "African Conversion." *Africa* 41 (1971): 87-108.

_____. "On the Rationality of Conversion." *Africa* 45 (1975): 219-235, 373-399.

Linden, Ian. *Catholics, Peasants and Chewa Resistance in Nyasaland*. Berkeley: University of California Press, 1974.

Little, Kenneth. "The Role of the Secret Society in Cultural Specialization." *American Anthropologist* 51 (1949): 199-212.

_____. "The Political Function of the Poro." *Africa* 35 (1965): 349-365 and 36 (1966): 62-72.

Malinowski, Bronislaw. *Magic, Science and Religion and Other Essays*. Anchor Books edition. N.Y.: Doubleday and Company, 1954.

Oliver. Roland. The Missionary Factor in East Africa. London: Longman Group Ltd., 1972.

Parkin, David. "Politics of Ritual Syncretism: Islam among the Non-Muslim Giriama of Kenya." Africa 40 (1970)

Peel, J.D.Y. Aladura: A Religious Movement among the Yoruba. London: Oxford University Press, 1969.

Radcliffe-Brown, A.R. Structure and Function in Primitive Society. N.Y.; The Free Press, 1965.

Ranger, Terence and Kimambo, Isaria. The Historical Study of African Religion. Berkeley: University of California Press, 1972.

Ranger, Terence and Weller, John. Themes in the Christian History of East and Central Africa. Berkeley: University of California Press, 1975.

Ray, Benjamin. African Religions: Symbols, Ritual and Community. Englewood Cliffs, N.J.: Prentice Hall Incorporated, 1976.

Rodney, Walter. A History of the Upper Guinea Coast. N.Y.: Monthly Review Press, 1970.

Strayer, Robert. The Making of Mission Communities in East Africa. London: Heinemann Educational Books Ltd., 1978.

Thomas, Keith. Religion and the Decline of Magic. N.Y.: Charles Scribner's Sons, 1971.

Turner, Victor. The Forest of Symbols. Ithaca, N.Y.: Cornell University Press, 1967.

_____. The Ritual Process. Ithaca, N.Y.: Cornell University Press, 1969.

_____. Dramas, Fields, and Metaphors. Ithaca, N.Y.: Cornell University Press, 1974.

Weber, Max. The Protestant Ethic and the Spirit of Capitalism. N.Y.: Charles Scribner's

Sons, 1958.

Wilson, Godfrey and Wilson, Monica. The Analysis of Social Change. Cambridge: Cambridge University Press, 1945.

Wilson, Monica. Religion and the Transformation of Society. London: Cambridge University Press, 1971.

Whisson, Michael G. and West Martin. Religion and Social Change. Cape Town: D. Philip, 1975.

INDEX

Allison, S.B., 151
Americo Liberians,
  attitudes towards
  Africans, 81-82, 85-87,
  144; kinship among, 82;
  political position and
  religion, 83-85;
  society, 80-83;
  settlements, 87-90
ancestor veneration
  (ngamua kweni), 51-54,
  61, 209-214.
Anderson, Benjamin, 93-94
Ashmun, Jehudi, 84
Bacon, Samuel, 83-84
Baptist Church, 85
Barclay, Pres. Arthur, 92
Barclay, Pres. Edwin, 117-119
Barclay, John, 123-124
"Big men", 20, 33-35, 39, 56
Bokomu, 100
Bopolu, 70, 73, 74, 88-89, 90
Bowers, Rev. Louis T.,
Carey, Lott, 84
Catholic White Fathers
  (Malawi), 138
causation, 41-44
Cheeseman, Pres. Joseph, 90-91
Chewa (Malawi), 138
chiefs, clan, 37;
  manipulation of system,
  113, 119; paramount,
  37; subchief, 37-38
Christian villages, 105-106
Christianity, as religion
  of dominant group, 4,
  223-224; and Kpelle
  religion, 141
Conversion, 137-139;
  mission strategies for,
  140-141, 143, 146, 199
Dagle, Rev. David, 152, 159, 160
district commissioners,
  92, 94-96, 115, 130
divination, kola nut, 46;
  sandplaying, 46-48
dreams, 45-46
Dubli, 94
Evangelical Lutheran
  Church in Liberia, 189-191
Fernando Po, 116-117
Firestone rubber
  plantation, 114, 117,
  127, 152, 177, 208, 222
food taboos, 61-62
Foreign Missionary Society
  (Lutheran), 102-103
Freemasonry among Americo
  Liberians, 83
Fuama, 69
Gbalein, 70, 123
Gbili (Giddings), 113-114, 119-120, 122, 125
Gbolomu (town), 167-168, 237
Geertz, Clifford, 3-4, 19-20,
General Synod (Lutheran), 102
Giddings family, 71-73, 76, 97, 113
Giddings, Peter, 120, 125-127, 129, 131, 132, 151, 174, 218
Giting, 97-101, 146-147, 149
God, Kpelle concept of,
  40, 48, 201-203, 207-208
Gola, 69, 70, 74, 88, 89
"half-towns", 71

heaven, 62, 203-204, 219
Horton, Robin, 227
Howard, Pres. Daniel, 98
indentured pupils, 103-104
indirect rule, 92
Islam, compared to Christianity, 224-225
Johkwele, 70, 112
Kakata, 94
Kilibe (town), 123
King, Pres. Charles, 117
kinship system, 28-29, 33, 39, 61-63, 213
Kpaiya, 100, 125
Kpelle, and Americo Liberians, 9, 22-23, 94-96; agriculture, 21-24; chiefdoms, 77; economy, 23, 33-35; history, 4-5, 21-22, 68-69, 93-96; importance, 93; kinship, 24,25; labor obligations, 25-26; land ownership, 24-25; marriage, 26-27, 34-35; medicine (sale),57-60, 216-218; political position, 37-38, 77; religion, 40-65; religion and Christianity, 141-142; slavery, 28; social groups, 20, 33, 39-40, 60; view of human nature, 44; women, 26-27, 32, 221, 229
Kpelle religion, 40-65, 139; and social groups 60-65
Kpolopelle Station, 107, 108
"kwi", 67, 208, 220-225
labor obligations, Kpelle 25-27; government, 114-116
labor recruitment, 114-116
Liberia, evangelical nature of founding, 6-8, 83-85; foreign pressure, 91, 94; history, 8-9, 69-70, 80; interior policy, 92-93, 109-110, 111, 112, 115, 117-119, 130; League of Nations slavery investigation, 116; opposition to founding, 7; "pacification" of Kpelle, 91, 112; reorganization of interior service, 117-119
Liberian Frontier Force, 92-93
literacy, and political office, 123-127, program, 178-179
Loma, 137
Lugard, Frederick, 92
Luther's Small Catechism, 162-166,
Lutheran mission, acceptance of African customs, 191; and Kpelle religion, 139-142; and Poro Society, 172-175; as bridge to Americo Liberian world, 130, 194-195; Bible texts used, 153-157, 162-168, 180-187; black evangelists, 106, 150, 189-191; changes after World War II, 177-197; conflicts with local leaders, 175-176; church membership statistics, 193-195; conversion strategies, 140-141, 143, 146, 156-157, 199; definition of conversion, 138-139, 195; evangelism program, 148-149, 153-159, 161-168, 172, 180-189; gifts, 145,148;

history, 101-103; in Liberia 103-108, in Sanoyea, 107, 135-137, 146-165; Kpelle language program, 178-179; literacy program, 179; medical program, 149-150; pressures facing converts, 167, 169-171; restrictions for converts, 172-175; schools, 103-105, 147-148, 152-153, 157; sought cultural transformation, 143-145, 178; tithing in Sanoyea, 160; turnover of personnel, 106, 150
Mande, 68-69
Mandinka, 69-70, 88-89
medicines (sale), 57-60, 216-218
Methodists, 85, 124, 137; in Malawi, 138
migration, 69-71
Mina (Witchfinding) Society, 36
"model for reality", 18, 199
"model of reality", 17, 40-44, 45, 199
Moling (spirit), 188; Society, 36
Muhlenberg Mission Station, 103-106
Muslims in Sanoyea, 100, 109, 121-123; relations with mission, 122-123
Officer, Morris, 103-104
Palakwele, 192
pawns, 114
Poro Society, 28-33, 35-36, 78-79, 131-133, 214-216, 225-227; and mission, 172-175
Presbyterian church, 85
Protestant Episcopal Mission, 85, 137, 138
Religion 64-65; and society 18-20; as technical mastery, 18; definition 16-17
Religious change, problems in identifying, 197-199; in concept of afterlife, 203-205; in concept of God, 202-203, 207-208; ritual change, 205-209; sociology of, 227-230
sacrifices, 49
Sande Society, 32-33
Sanoyea, bypassed by road, 177; history 70, 73-75, 76-80, 96; mission, 07, 146-199; political elite, 123-126; Poro grove, 131-133; ties with Americo Liberians, 127-130
schools (mission), 103-105, 147-148, 152-153, 157
Siwi (Wockpaling), 76-77, 79-80, 97
slavery, 28, 75, 76, 114, 125, 151
spirits, 48-49; birth, 50-51; dream, 50, nature, 50, 207-209; of the dead, 51-54; personal, 49, 207-208; water people, 54
Stewart, Albert, 107, 150-151
taxes, 113-114, 116
Todi, 69, 94
Toosolung, 71-72
Totota, 177, 179
Town rituals, 63, 218-219
trade, 69-70, 81, 88-89, 90, 96-97
Turner, Victor, 2-3
Vai, 69, 76
Wallahun, 97, 99
war, 73-75, 76
Welmers, William, 13, 178
Westerman, Diedrich, 13, 178
Wilson, Monica, 227
witchcraft, 55-57, 200-201
Zota, 70
Zulu Hills, 94

AFRICAN STUDIES

1. Karla Poewe, **The Namibian Herero: A History of their Psychosocial Disintegration and Survival**
2. Sara Joan Talis, **Oral Histories of Three Secondary School Students in Tanzania**
3. Randolph Stakeman, **The Cultural Politics of Religious Change: A Study of the Sanoyea Kpelle in Liberia**